Brave Lion

Brave Lion

The life, journeys and adventures of
Gholam Hussein Paksima

AHMAD PAKSIMA

ReadersMagnet, LLC

The Brave Lion: The life, journeys and adventures of Gholam Hussein Paksima
Copyright © 2023 by Ahmad Paksima

Published in the United States of America
ISBN   Paperback: 978-1-960629-51-7
ISBN   Hardback: 978-1-960629-52-4
ISBN   eBook: 978-1-960629-53-1

All rights reserved. No part of this publication may be reproduced, stored in a retrieval system or transmitted in any way by any means, electronic, mechanical, photocopy, recording or otherwise without the prior permission of the author except as provided by USA copyright law.

The opinions expressed by the author are not necessarily those of ReadersMagnet, LLC.

ReadersMagnet, LLC
10620 Treena Street, Suite 230 | San Diego, California, 92131 USA
1.619. 354. 2643 | www.readersmagnet.com

Book design copyright © 2023 by ReadersMagnet, LLC. All rights reserved.

Cover design by Ericka Obando
Interior design by Dorothy Lee

TABLE OF CONTENTS

Foreword 11

The First Connection - Amritsar, India 13

Discovering A Legend 16

The Story As Narrated By Mr. Ahmad Paksima 18

Tracing The Family Roots 21

Remembering The Past 26

The Beginning Of A New Era - A Turning Point 35

Travels & Future Events 41

The Amir Of Bukhara Mohammad, Alum Ali Khan 52

Clash Of Principles 60

The Pains Of Progress 65

The Rangoon Episode 71

The Revolution In Iran 74

Family Tree 75

Purchase Of The Village Of Fatehabad 78

The Emergence Of India Coffee House 83

E Muratore, The Italian Restaurant 89

Association Of Gholam Hussein With Key Personalities 103

Chiang Kai-Shek - Former President Of Taiwan 105

Mohammad Ali Jinnah 107

C. K. Naydu 108

The B. K. S. Iyenger Connection 111

Revisiting The Roots 113

A Final Journey To A Native Land 114

Links To The Prithvi Raj Chauhan Dynasty 117

Gholam Hussein Paksima

Dedication Page

~~~

I would like to dedicate this book to my brothers Kazem Paksima, Ali Paksima, Mahmood Paksima, sisters Esmat, Seema, and all my relatives and friends who gave me valuable suggestions in compiling this book.

Foreword

It is with a feeling of excitement and joy that I am writing this foreword for my friend, Ahmad Paksima, his family and his brothers and sisters and their families. After years of persuasion, I have put together the story of Gholam Hussein Paksima. It has always been an arduous task to prevail upon his family members to narrate the life events of their father.

I understand that it is neither proper nor justified to extol the virtues of this book that you are holding in your hands, although I am tempted to do so — the primary reason being my admiration for the Paksima family and the devoted pride with which I have always hung on to every detail for the last two decades we have been together.

From the wolf-whistling front benchers, to the most serious critics, Gholam Hussein Paksima's varied range of repertoires aroused a spontaneous admiration from his friends and family. The poignant, as well as the mirthful experiences as Mr. Ahmad narrates about his father, gives you an insight into the making of a great character called Gholam Hussein Paksima.

When I first heard the story of this great man from his grandson, Shahram Paksima, and later on from his son, Mr. Ahmad Paksima, it was the characters that first captured my imagination. They were fascinating people whose stories were highly dramatic. The real life drama in Gholam Hussein Paksima's life, the turbulence of various developments in his life, and the agony of ruthless struggle for survival simply provided the canvas on which is told a moving and highly personal story of endeavor and success.

By putting the pieces together, a magisterial real life drama was crafted which portrayed the agony of relentless struggle, the complexity of passion, and the invincibility of the human spirit.

The ambitious visions coupled with emotional magnitude — their transformation into ultimate reality is an exceptional illustration of human achievements.

I want the entire Paksima family to be acquainted with the incidents and episodes in this book and to feel for themselves Gholam Hussein's genius, straight-forwardness, and immeasurable goodness of heart. His persona transcends everything - lands, religions, and castes. He had an aura of greatness and class which made him stand out in a gathering everywhere, be it at home, in a family get-together, or a formal business party amidst people of high lineage in a royal palace. To say that he was citizen of the world is certainly no tall claim.

It was not the easiest assignment of my life for sure. As my conversation with Mr. Ahmad and his brother, Mr. Kazem continued, the real picture began to emerge. I began to see the unfolding of his saga like the scenes in a movie. As Mr. Ahmad narrated his father's story, I noticed how much he enjoyed the recapitulation of his childhood years in the village where he could feel the pain that his father had undergone while taking most challenging decisions of his life and the repercussions as well.

In our conversations, Mr. Ahmad relates the events that changed the life of his father. He traces his journey right from his childhood to the end. He candidly recounts his interactions and relations with a wide variety of people and also from other walks of life, including politicians and celebrities.

I have tried to reconstruct the events by listening to the recorded conversations and interviews with Mr. Ahmad and his relatives and in doing so, I have checked up details from all available sources without forsaking the historical accuracy.

Nirmal Singh Dhiman

The First Connection - Amritsar, India

It was in the summer of 1996 when I met Shahram Paksima, a young American, at Golden Temple, Amritsar in the evening during the final prayers of the day. I was curious about the thorough concentration and interest that he was showing in the temple. I could instantly judge that he was an intellectual young student. I introduced myself and started a conversation about Punjab, its people, culture, and role of religious organizations in the field of education.

Shahram Paksima told me that he intended to stay at Amritsar for about 15 days and his mission was to study the role of the management committee of the Temple in the field of education and Panchayati Raj system in India. His in-depth knowledge in various fields and an understanding of human values impressed me so much that we became instant friends.

I offered Shahram my house at Amritsar to stay which was close to the Golden Temple which he accepted gracefully on the condition that we would be discussing the various subjects every day for a few hours so that he could have a better understanding of the Indian society, its culture, and educational system. This was part of his academic assignment as he was pursuing a master's degree from Brigham Young University, Utah in Public Policy.

During the course of his stay at Amritsar, we literally discussed everything, sharing our perceptions about the two opposing cultures, their values, and their humanitarian involvements. His father, Mr. Ahmad Paksima, was running a business in San

Diego, California and he was very pleased to know about our relationship which eventually turned out to be very personal one.

Mr. Ahmad Paksima was interested to find out the roots of his family, especially his ancestors who hailed from Punjab, India. His forefathers were from Punjab and he advised Shahram to visit his ancestral village, Khosa Pando in Moga with me to find out details of his family history and his ancestors. We made a trip to the village, Khosa Pando in Moga, where his father, Mr. Veer Singh, grandfather of Shahram, was born and spent the early years of his life back in early 1900s. We went to the village and met people who were connected to the family and knew a little bit about Veer Singh. We were able to get some interesting information about Veer Singh and the circumstances which influenced him to leave the village to pursue his dreams for a better future.

Later, in 1998, Mr. Ahmad came to India for a personal visit and we met each other at Amritsar for the first time. We discussed his ancestors in detail based on whatever information he had and decided to go to Khosa Pando Village at Moga to seek more information. His stay in India was for a few days only and before leaving we decided that we might be able to get some genealogy records from Haridwar. I was given this assignment.

Haridwar is a place where his ancestors used to go for the final rites of their deceased and here, the priests keep records of the ancestors dating back to 15th century. The record comprises of the date of death, people who visited the place for final rites, and records of their siblings. I continued my search for the details of ancestors by visiting Haridwar several times and I have detailed those visits and information that I was able to extract from there in the latter part of this writing.

I migrated to Canada in January 2000 and Mr. Ahmad helped me a lot to settle down in many ways. Mr. Ahmad was born in Bombay, India in 1940 but his father, Veer Singh, had moved to Karachi and later to Iran and settled over there permanently. During his life, Mr. Veer Singh had travelled to many countries and his life was an inspiring story of struggle, motivation, and hard work. It was so impressive and inspirational that we decided to seek more details about his eventful life. We wanted to record his life that was so full of adventures and achievements for others to read and see for themselves as a model of exemplary courage and motivation executed with relentless struggle in life.

Mr. Ahmad was seriously considering exploring the detailed events of his father's life which were a source of inspiration to him throughout his life. He had discussed this with his brothers and sisters who encouraged him to further search for events and circumstances which Veer Singh had encountered. Mr. Ahmad suggested that I should come to San Diego and stay with him for a couple of days to scrutinize and research the historical events that his father had gone through in his life. He had some audio tapes which had a recorded conversation with his father back in 1973 during their visit to India. Knowing the importance of the conversation, Mr. Ahmad recorded it so that he could further search the events in chronological order. We together started to put the pieces together to find out more details about the life of Veer Singh. Listening to the tapes, we found out a lot of information about the life of a person who was born in an ordinary family, in a rather underdeveloped village of Punjab, and brought up in an ordinary manner, yet who went on to become an extraordinary man through his sheer courage, audacity, and skilful planning. The more we listened to the tapes (that revealed the journey of Veer Singh's life), it became clear that it was the story of a man who was not an ordinary person but a man of vision, ambition, and someone who planned his future with uncanny precision and courage. There are few people who change the history of their family and Veer Singh was one of them. He was always ahead of his time!

Discovering a Legend

Here, we have the story of Veer Singh as narrated by Mr. Ahmad Paksima based on his conversations, observations, records, interviews, and historical substantiation.

"My Dad, Mr. Veer Singh, has always been a source of inspiration to me and has remained my mentor. I had always wanted my children, brothers, sisters, and my grandchildren to know about this great man who made his way to the United States through relentless hard work and sheer planning. My purpose of writing this book is to recount the legacy that his grandchildren now possess, to perceive his achievements, and how he single-handedly accomplished success and established a better future for them. It will be fair to highlight his style of working, dealing with the toughest phases of life, and eventually attaining success and recognition. He was instrumental in creating a ground from where we all could grow further. He did it with his genius and courage.

I would like to add here that in terms of sheer audacity, if nothing else, the travelogue and adventures of legendary explorers have been highlighted and depicted in movies that are a treat to watch for many. The same can be said of my dad, Veer Singh.

Throughout his life, he was a man of amazing courage, and his ambitions were well-planned. That is why he remains a source of constant motivation for our family and others who knew him."

This is not just a family history or narration of his life events. It is a story which leaves many inspirational thoughts, an illustration of how one can reach heights with sheer determination as he did in his life.

This is an inside look at one man's rise to the heights of fame, fortune, recognition, and an inevitable rags-to-riches saga.

It is also a story of agony of inadequate means, resources, complexity of passion, relationship, and invincibility of the human spirit.

This story describes the immense struggle a man in his pursuit for fulfilment of his ambitions and eventual settlement in life in the most remarkable style. It speaks of his overcoming insurmountable obstacles, with unrestrained passion and obsession, defeating the outrageous plans orchestrated by his enemies and competitors.

It is the story of an under-privileged young boy who had very little schooling, yet he learned many languages and became far more prudent than many intellectuals. His approach to life, pursuit for perfection and success remained thoroughly centred and never allowed his passions to distract from his eventual goals. In his relentless search for success, and survival, he travelled to many different countries for fulfilment of his plans, coupled with his amazing ability. He started his mission repeatedly with no money or assets. With nothing acquired in inheritance in terms of money or property, he built his own future for his offspring.

Whereas others dream in life for a successful career and fortune, he created it entirely on his own.

His life story involves a series of struggle, overcoming obstacles, and endurance. He is a source of inspiration for his children and others and yet a very little is known about him to other people of the present generation. There is a lot to learn from his lifestyle, his complex way of handling difficult situations, and also his deep interest in academic knowledge — something that he missed in his childhood.

The Story as Narrated by Mr. Ahmad Paksima

My father, Veer Singh, was born in the village of Roop Nagar near Moga District, Punjab in the year 1898. Ascertaining the year of his birth has remained a challenge but this seems to be the most accurate. His father, Mehtab Singh, was a simple farmer having few acres of land. The family had moved to the village of Roop Nagar because of some natural disasters in the village but returned to Khosa Pando in 1902. It is not known as to what had caused this migration, but it is presumed that it was due to the floods that forced many villagers of Khosa Pando to move. Later, when the conditions in Khosa Pando had improved, the family returned to their native village.

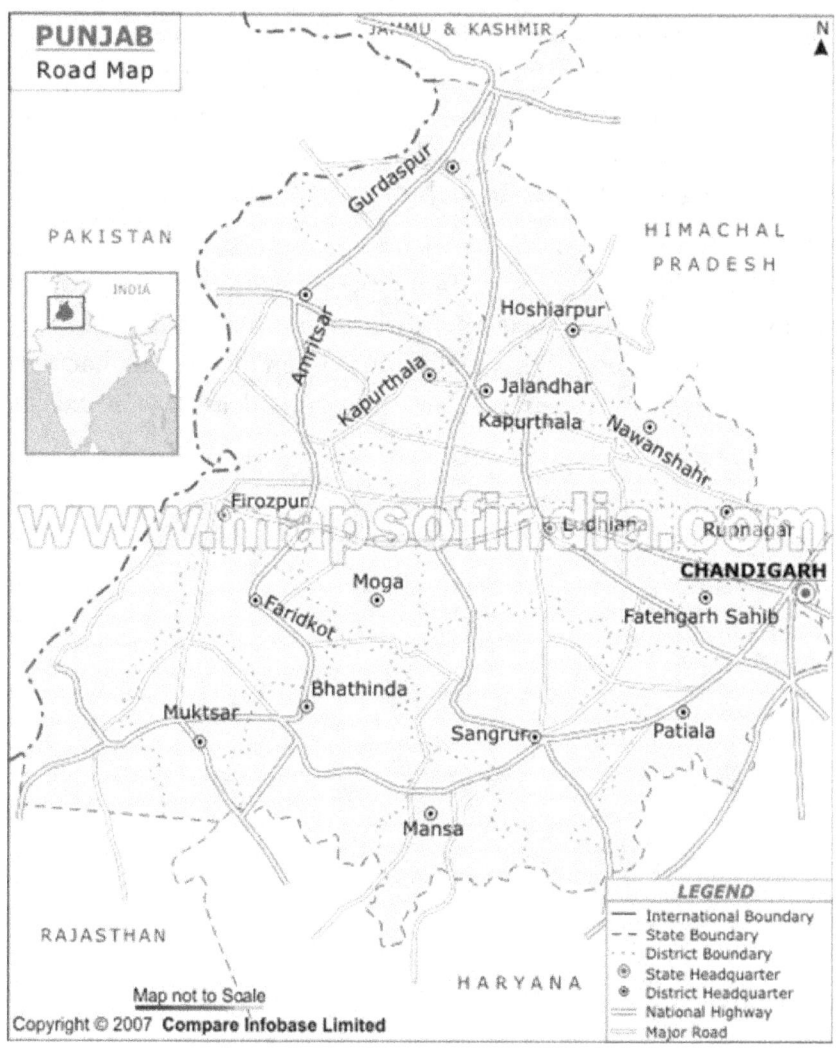

This is a map of Punjab.
The village Khosa Pando is in Moga District.

Veer Singh's father was a Sikh by religion but his mother was a Hindu. His father, Mehtab Singh, owned agriculture land — not a substantial area of land, but enough to live moderately. Mehtab Singh had one brother named Dasonda Singh who had never married. Dasonda Singh was a man of eccentric character. He never took any interest in the family farming business and would often disappear from the village to return after several months. On one occasion, he left the village, never to come back again and nothing was heard about him even though a lot of search was made.

In the village, there were many people who were addicted to opium. Mehtab Singh was one of them and he continued selling his property because of this addiction. When he died, he had very little land left to his name. The year of his death is not exactly known.

Tracing the Family Roots

In an attempt to find out details of the ancestors of the family, we went to Haridwar in India to get this information from the priests who maintain family records. These priests record the names of ancestors in their books. After making persistent efforts, we were able to get the record dating back from 1644 AD onwards. The priest who performed final rites for the people of village Khosa Pando provided this record from his books that were hundreds of years old. It is by tradition that one particular priest would be keeping record of a specific area and pass it on to his family. In return, they expect a donation for their services in order for them to make a living.

Haridwar, located in North India, is a place where the sacred river Ganga flows. The 2,510 km river rises in the Western Himalayas in the Uttarakhand state of India and drains into the Sunderbans Delta in the Bay of Bengal. It has long been considered a holy river by Hindus and worshiped as the goddess *Ganga* in Hinduism. It has also been an important place historically. Many former provincial or imperial capitals (such as Patliputra, Kannauj, Kara, Allahabad, Murshidabad, and Calcutta) have been located on its banks. Ganga and its tributaries drain a 1,000,000 square-kilometre fertile basin that supports one of the world's highest densities of humans. The average depth of the river is 52 feet, and the maximum depth is around 100 feet.

For centuries, Hindus have been visiting the holy town of Haridwar for pilgrimage, and the post-cremation rites of their dead that include the immersion of the ashes and bones of their deceased into the waters of the river Ganga as followed by Hindu religious customs. It has been a centuries-old tradition to visit the Pandit who is in charge of one's family history records so that he would register and update the family's genealogical record. Since there were no government agencies to register such records, the records of these priests are legally acceptable.

Modernization and digitization of records has however changed all of this.

While Hindus continue to visit Haridwar for the final rites, sikhs prefer Kiratpur (near Chandigarh) where they have a Gurudwara, or a Sikh Temple named Patalpuri as a destination for final rites. They don't have priests at the Gurudwara like they have in Haridwar. The Sikh Gurudwara is located on the bank of a river and a priest in the Sikh temple just says a prayer and records it in their register.

It is important to understand how these priests maintain the records and to what extent they are authentic. When someone dies in the family, he is cremated according to Hindu rites and it is a religious practice to immerse the ashes and bones at Haridwar in the Ganga River. One particular district or several villages in that area is managed by one priest who would keep the records. These records are systematically maintained by classifying their castes according to the caste of the deceased and their provenance. For instance, Gill clans of Moga District will have one single priest who has been maintaining the death records. When we started enquiring about the keeper of the records from Moga District, it was not difficult to find him. Sometimes, this family business is divided further on the basis of castes. For each caste or a clan, a different book is maintained which is further classified according to the villages falling under its jurisdiction. It is, therefore, fairly easy for them to locate the family history. It was amazing to see that the record contained the names of people who visited for the final rites of their dear ones, their signatures, and the amount of donation given. When we made our enquiries, we were pleasantly surprised to find the names of Ahmad, his wife, Shahram, and other family members in the genealogy records.

These priests insist that the present generation of people should come to them and get their records updated by providing all relevant details regarding their present address, names of their spouse and children as well. Even the visitors who come to collect information on someone else's behalf are required to sign.

When we approached the priest in charge of the Khasa Pando records for details regarding Veer Singh's ancestors, we were asked to provide details of Veer Singh's siblings, then all the records were updated. The Pandit named Chander Parkash had recorded all the details of the present Paksima family.

The record of Khosa Pando had been traditionally kept by Pandit Moti Ram known as Boharwale (tree side), his office being close to Hanuman Temple, Haridwar. Pandit Moti Ram had passed away 80 years back and his sons and grandsons were now managing this business. Presently, Moti Ram's son, Pandit Ganga Prasad, and his son, Chander Parkash, maintain all the records dating back to 1200 AD. The letter from Pandit Ganga Prasad is reproduced below. Based on the record provided by the priest at Haridwar, the family tree of Veer Singh would appear like this:

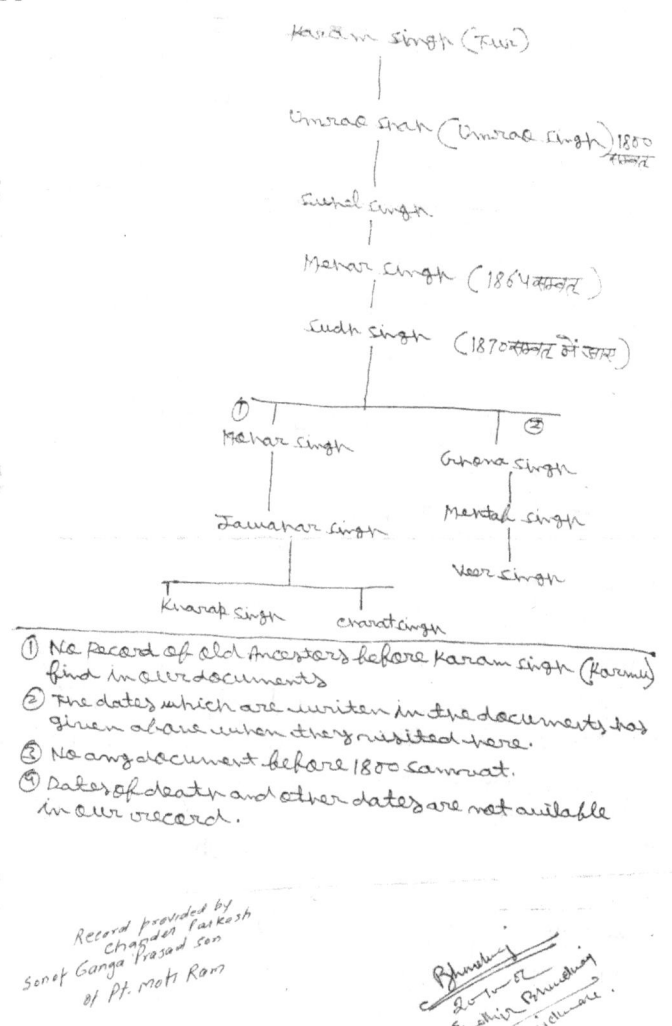

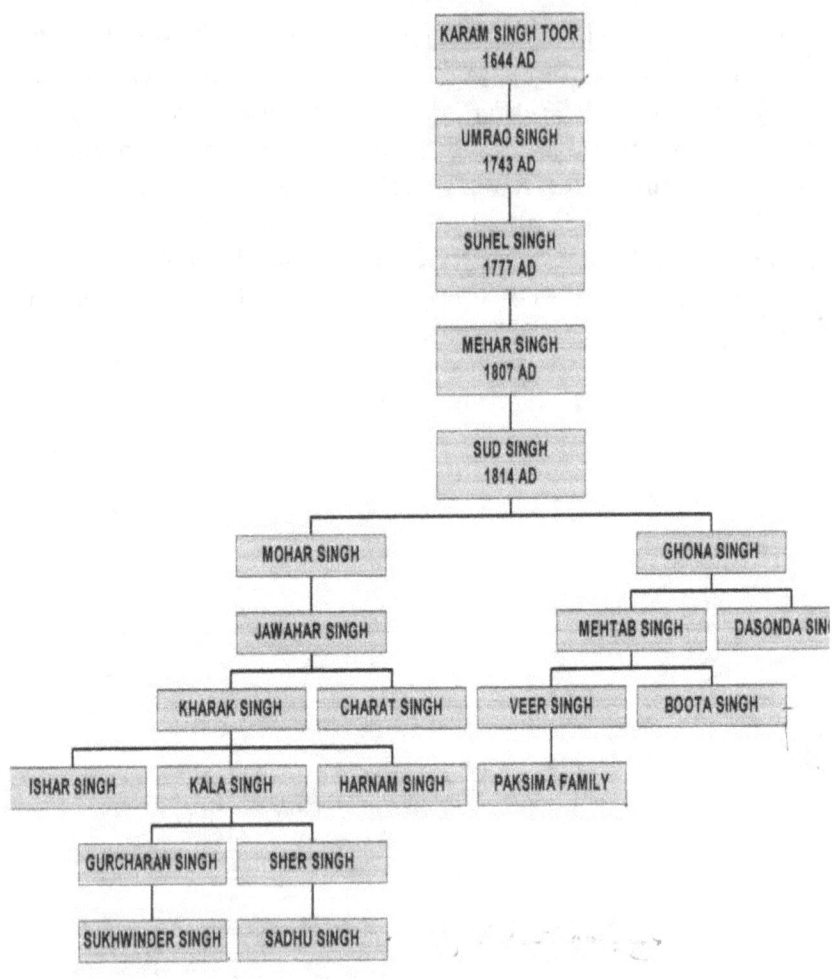

FAMILY TREE OF PAKSIMA FAMILY

On the basis of the ancestral record of the family as provided by the Pandit in Haridwar, it was in 1644 AD when Karam Singh Toor was converted to Sikhism. Mehtab Singh, father of Veer Singh, had two sons and two daughters:

1. Mehtabi   -   Daughter
2. Boota Singh   -   Eldest Son
3. Name not known -   Daughter
4. Veer Singh   -   Son

Mehtabi, the eldest daughter was married to Dhan Singh, a numberdar (high official who keeps land records) at the village Pakkhi Sardaran, now known as Pakhi Kalan. This village is close to Khosa Pando in Faridkot District. Dhan Singh had one brother named Sham Singh who was a highly placed official serving the Maharaja of Faridkot.

In fact, the Faridkot District was ruled by a king (Maharaja) named Gurdarshan Singh who, in order to win favours from the British regime, would strictly follow the orders of British rulers and would go to any limit to please them. He was cruel towards his people and tried to ruthlessly suppress anyone who participated in India's freedom struggle. One prominent opponent to the king was a political leader, Giani Zail Singh, from Faridkot who later became president of India, one of the most accomplished and shrewd politicians that India has produced. It appears that Sham Singh was working for this Maharaja. The ruler of Faridkot had his own army.

Mehtabi, sister of Veer Singh, had two sons named Inder Singh and Mohinder Singh, along with two daughters (names not known). We don't have any information about the whereabouts of this family. Dhan Singh had served in the army at the Pakhi Sardaran military camp where he was a top ranking officer and very close to the king. The relations between the Veer Singh family and Dhan Singh family became strained later on the occasion of marriage of Mehtabi's daughter. Veer Singh and his mother arrived with a water buffalo to be given as a wedding present. It was a custom during those days to present a buffalo as a gift and though it was quite expensive during those days, Dhan Singh's family was not happy as they were expecting more and they refused to accept it. Aggrieved by this, Veer Singh and his mother were upset and left the village without attending the ceremony.

Remembering the Past

Veer Singh narrated how his father used to plough the land the traditional way. In his own words, "We had two other workers who would help us. At home, we had a simple life, with a dog whose name was Damri (meaning one paisa or cent) and the usual domestic animals and cattle."

In one conversation, Veer Singh stated, "My mother was a very kind-hearted lady, and she took care of me very lovingly. In fact, I was very beloved to her in the family and she used to tell me fairy tales."

Veer Singh went on to tell me in his own words, "I was very inquisitive and would be asking questions endlessly, and sometimes she had no answers. I just kept on pondering and looking for answers."

During his early years, he spoke about Sham Singh who worked as a high official at the King's Darbar. In his own words, "I remember once, our family was invited to watch a play in the official palace of the king where Sham Singh had authority. I was curious to see the king and from a distance, I saw him sitting on a luxurious highchair which was placed above other chairs. There was a theatre in his court and the famous English play, "A Pound of Flesh" by Shakespeare, was enacted. The play impressed me a lot and I kept on thinking about the king, his palace, and the luxury that he enjoyed."

I silently had wishful thinking. I wished that I, too, could possess power, fame, luxury, and style like the king did. I kept on wondering how God had created so much disparity. In 1905, there was a big earthquake in North-eastern Himachal Pradesh which shook the village very badly. This was one of biggest earthquakes of the century with a magnitude of 7.8, killing nearly 19,800 people.

He told me in his own words, "I remember very clearly that when this huge earthquake of such a magnitude occurred, our dog, Damri, was alarmed beforehand, and my mother wrapped me in a blanket."

Later, when the tremors subsided, he was curious to know what had caused the earthquake and asked his mother. "How could such terrible shaking happen?" Veer Singh was stunned by this strange phenomenon. It was quite shocking to him but his mother did not have any logical answers to his intriguing questions.

There was no water supply in the houses at that time. My mother would go to the nearby well to get water and before leaving, she would lock me in a room and instructed me not to go out. The only source of water for the household use was the well and we had to store water for our needs.

In the days to come, Veer Singh's brother, Boota Singh, had a severe attack of pneumonia and he passed away after struggling for a few days. This incident further shocked his father. He felt very depressed and in agony, he would often cry.

"My back has been broken and I am literally left alone," his father would often say and he too was sad to see him in shock. He did not know what he meant. He would console him and say, "Father, I am going to massage your back and your pain will go away." He felt that his back had some serious problem and because of which, he was in pain.

Veer Singh loved his father very much. He also had very deep affection for his brother, Boota Singh. Both the brothers were close to each other as Boota Singh was very caring and Veer Singh respected him very much.

There was no book to read in the house. He came to know about the existence of dictionaries much later. He realised that it was a book which contained all the English words. He learned from the environment, the stories old farmers told, or songs that women sang at the daily spinning session or at the wedding. He also learned a lot from the Mirasins, the Muslim hereditary singers who drummed, danced, and sang at every ceremony.

The village had no school and the only nearest one was located six kilometres away in the nearby village named Saleena. His close friends, Suraj Mal and Rattan Singh, accompanied him to school. They would be together in school and participate in games. The heat during the summer was intense and it was hard to walk for such a long distance. It would take two hours to reach the school. The rubber soles of their shoes would often heat up, burning their feet and they were forced to take them off to relieve their feet for some time. They walked fast on the burning ground so that their feet were more in the air than on the ground.

He learnt the basics of the Punjabi language and wanted to continue his studies. He was quick to learn the lessons and knew that through education, he would be able to get answers to his questions. His father was proud of his going to school and often bragged to the villagers about his son going to school and doing well in studies.

His dad often proudly said, "My son is going to school and there he will attain knowledge and wisdom because he likes to acquire knowledge and someday, he will attain a high position in life." Few students went to school in those days.

Even at Saleena village, the school was up to primary level. The need for education was not considered a priority. People preferred to send their children to work in fields and schooling was not encouraged. One of the reasons for this was extreme poverty and limited resource. Besides, the government had no infrastructure for schooling.

While he was studying in the school, he would see maps, pictures of British kings, and the rulers of the state. When he looked at the map, he found the name of Karachi which fascinated him. There were pictures of animals, parrots, elephants, and lions that intrigued his curiosity. But he was more interested in exploring maps, getting to understand how big the world was and its vastness. He wanted to go where no one had gone before, to explore places that no one had dared to visit.

He wondered why his village Khosa Pando did not figure in the map. Even the city of Faridkot appeared as a tiny dot. He asked his teacher questions about cities, states, and countries. He came to know that the world was a huge place. There were cities much bigger than Faridkot, with a population of millions, and also they had life that moved at a terrific pace compared to Faridkot or Moga. These big cities had an entirely different lifestyle, which was fast and breathtakingly busy. Everyone seemed to be in a rush to overtake others. It was full of people with endless opportunities, challenges, and severe competition.

During this period, the British were ruling India and he would see British officers well-dressed and having expensive things with them. He wondered how these people could have access to the most expensive articles that he did not possess. When he asked his father as to how these people were able to afford all the luxuries of life, his father replied that these people had studied in schools and colleges, and they had worked hard in their profession and businesses and achieved success because of their intelligence and resources.

But his schooling went on only for 9 months. (This needs to be verified.) He had the biggest tragedy in life. His father became sick and had a massive attack of pneumonia. Despite getting treatment, he could not survive.

Veer Singh was left alone with his mother and there was no one to support the family. He had to give up schooling much against his wishes. However, he had learned Punjabi and Urdu well.

Life changed dramatically for Veer Singh and there was no choice for him but to work with his mother. Although they had some relatives in the village, Veer Singh and his mother did not seek anyone's help and continued to cope with the circumstances. For Veer Singh, life was monotonous and repetitious and without any future goal. He wondered what his future would be. He often discussed with his friends about future plans but none of them had any interest or dreams for the future.

There were many people from the village who had gone abroad to places like China and Singapore, in their search for better jobs and more money. One such person was Bagha who had gone to Singapore to try his luck. Bagha's job had eventually taken him to Japan where he met Hakim Hashim Ali. Bagha had rheumatism and he met Hakim in Japan who was a doctor in ophthalmology. He was originally from Iran and had studied in the USA. His father, Abu Ali, was also a doctor. But Hakim Hashim Ali also specialized in other medical fields. He successfully treated Bagha with all his experience and Bagha was very grateful to him for the special care that he had provided to him. He became a devoted admirer of Hakim and invited him to his village, Khosa Pando, when he would be back in India. Hakim promised that he would come to the village and meet him.

Bagha returned to his village after finishing his job. By this time, Hakim Hashim Ali was also back in Karachi after his travels from Japan and Singapore. Hakim had a passion for travelling and always wanted to see different parts of the world. Being a qualified and experienced medical practitioner, he always managed to establish himself wherever he went. Not only did it earn him money in the process, but it also provided him the opportunity to see different parts of the world.

Bagha was in touch with Hakim through mail and requested Hakim Hashim Ali to visit his village, Khosa Pando, and be his guest. Hakim had settled down at Karachi during the period of undivided India. Hakim accepted the invitation and agreed to see him at his village. Bagha was very happy that Hakim had accepted his invitation and he wanted to give him the best treatment at his visit. He told the villagers about Hakim. Everyone in the village was curious to see him.

Hakim arrived at the village in a taxi. Bagha was delighted and people from the village flocked to his house to see him. Hiring a taxi was not common as only rich people could afford and this was considered a symbol of affluence.

Veer Singh was excited when he got the news about the visit of the high-profile doctor. He was impressed by Hakim's personality and his lavish lifestyle. Veer Singh found the opportunity to talk to Hakim and showed great respect for him through his cool manners. He made sure that he was treated well. He took extra care and showed a lot of respect for Hakim.

Veer Singh could not sleep that night. Many thoughts crept in his mind, and he began to see life in a different way. *If Hakim could make his way to this incredible successful level, why can't I?* He started imagining the ways to achieve his goals. The whole thing seemed next to impossible because of his limited resources and personal liabilities. The circumstances were not in his favour, and it seemed a distant dream. The whole thing was agonizing, exasperating, and out of his reach.

But Veer Singh was not a person to give up easily or accept failure. It simply provided him more courage and he began to visualize a plan of action that could be turning point in his life. He needed someone who could be his mentor and provide him the opportunity to make a start in life.

He met Hakim regularly and asked him questions about his projects, travels, and at the same time pampering him with lot of respect, and assuring him of his loyalty. Hakim was impressed by his sincerity and when Veer Singh asked him for his address in Karachi, Hakim gave him his address and told him to visit him if he ever happened to be there. Hakim knew that Veer Singh might never be able to reach him but he did not want to discourage him. However, little did Hakim realize that this young boy was extremely ambitious and some day he would be his close associate.

In another incident, a person named Sham Singh returned from Singapore. He was lavishly dressed, wore an expensive watch, and had luxurious items from foreign countries. Veer Singh met Sham Singh, and this encouraged him further to pursue his dreams by any means. Now he was determined to take a calculated risk and move to a bigger city where he could start his life afresh and try his luck. The challenge was already written large on his mind.

Veer Singh felt that in order to be successful in life, he would have to accept great challenges, move to a bigger city and maybe Hakim in Karachi could be the right person to help him in his search for a placement in a world of opportunities and challenges. He was also aware of the fact that it was futile to convince his friends in this matter as they were content in living in a comfort zone of the kind of life they had. They did not have ambitions like him.

Pandit Suraj Mal had an argument with him on these issues but in the end, Pandit would end up believing that destiny was pre-planned by some mysterious force in heaven and he would get what was in store for him regardless of any effort, planning, or constructive action on his part.

Pandit said, "You know, we are all governed by a supreme being who controls the destiny of all individuals. If hard work, as they say, is the key to success, why do we have poor people in the world? Besides, it is too early to think about these things. Let us enjoy the present. We will see when there is a right time for this." "But we cannot achieve anything in this small village where we don't have any opportunity for a better future. At least, we shall have to make an attempt to grab opportunities and try our luck," Veer Singh replied.

"My dad has my horoscope, and he was telling me that we shall have great prosperity and good fortune in the village. We will have fame and respect in life in the village. He is never wrong in his predictions. It is sad you don't believe in the science of astrology. Trust me, it is all about the movement of the stars and our fate is determined by these stars." Pandit tried to convince Veer Singh.

But Veer Singh was not satisfied by this vague mythology. Veer Singh silently began to make plans for his future course of action and decided to go to Karachi to meet Hakim. He had the address of his residence in Karachi. This would be the beginning of his plans.

For a lad of just 9 years of age, without having seen much of the world outside his village, it was an enormous challenge. But now, he was determined to make a move and there was nothing that could stop him. He needed some money for his travelling to Karachi and living expenses there but he had no money with him. He understood his limits and disastrous consequences if his plans did not work well.

Veer Singh's younger sister was yet to be married. His mother had saved some money for her marriage but that was not enough. His mother asked him to buy a buffalo in the market and gave him Rs. 1000/- in cash for making this purchase. Veer Singh could not resist the temptation and his desire to make a move overcame him although it was the toughest moment for him — a decision that would always haunt him for the rest of his life. He told his mother that he would go to the city the next day. He planned to run away with the money.

That night was the hardest for Veer Singh. He could not sleep the whole night reflecting over his decision. What exactly would be his plan of action? How would his friends and relatives react to this and how would he face the stigma for the rest of his life? He was utterly baffled. There was no one he could talk to about this. He silently began to pray and asked God to help him. He also had the apprehension that there was no guarantee that Hakim would help him. The whole situation was too precarious. Deeply thinking about the unknown future, sleep overtook him.

He woke up in the early morning feeling nervous and confused. He recited his prayers and finally felt that it was a now-or-never opportunity. He decided to leave the house and avail of the opportunity with the confidence that he would return the money shortly once he started earning in Karachi and eventually take his mother with him and she would not have to work the way she was doing in the village. He must take this step to advance his life.

Without disclosing his plans to anyone, much less his friends, he went to the market to "buy the buffalo." He had 1000/- rupees for this and secured it in his pocket. He left the village carrying nothing with him, never to return. From the Mandi (market), he boarded a bus to Ferozepur from where he was to board a train to Ambala and though nervous and confused, he spent a couple of hours at the railway station gazing at the busy crowd, something he had rarely seen before.

The Beginning of a New Era - A Turning Point

While he was sitting there, lonely, a policeman on patrol came to him and asked him, "Hey, what are you doing here? Where do you have to go?"

To this he replied, "I have to go to Multan to see my brother. I am waiting for the train."

"Have you purchased the ticket?" policeman asked.

"No, I have yet to buy one."

Veer Singh was disturbed.

"Can you tell me where to get the ticket?"

"It seems you have never travelled before. Come with me. I will show you," responded the policeman.

Veer Singh had some change but not enough for the ticket. In a surprising gesture, the policeman paid the balance from his own pocket out of sheer compassion. He advised him to take a rest and wait for the train to Multan as it would take some time to arrive.

Finally, the train arrived on time, and he got into it, still in a state of panic and anxiety. He checked his pocket from time to time to ensure that the money was safe. He did not feel like eating anything. The thoughts of his village, his mother, relatives, and friends that he had left behind kept on haunting him.

But now there was no chance of a reversal of plans. He tried to occupy his mind with positive thoughts, hoping that everything would turn out well.

The train finally reached Multan from where he had to take another train that would take him to his destination - Karachi. It was a low-fare ordinary passenger train which stopped at every station on its way. It would take 12 hours more than an express train. Finally, the train reached Karachi. He was hungry, not having eaten enough in the train.

After getting some tea and a frugal meal, he got out of the railway station to find out where Hakim was living. He had his address written on a piece of paper. It was a big city with a multitude of people; everyone seemed to be in haste — quick and busy. He asked many people about the locality of the house. Finally, he reached the colony, and he saw one lady who was washing clothes. She immediately sensed that this boy was new in town and looking for some address.

"Where do you want to go? Who are you looking for?" asked the lady.

Veer Singh explained that he was looking for Hakim Hashim Ali and his house should be in this locality.

The lady exclaimed "You are at the right spot. I know this person. In fact, I work at his house. I will take you inside. Does he know you?" she asked.

"Yes, I have come from Punjab, and I have to see him. He was at my village sometime back and that is where I first met him," he replied.

Hakim, who was staying in a bungalow with his mother and sister, was extremely surprised to see Veer Singh.

"My God, how come you are here? What are you doing here?" Hakim was surprised. He could not believe that a village teenager would make it to his house to meet him. He remembered that Veer Singh was keen to come to Karachi and he had promised to get him a job in Karachi.

"I have come here all the way from my village, and I have decided to settle down in Karachi. I will work here, find a job, no matter how small but I will work hard and live honestly. I did not see any future in the village life. I even had to abandon my education and now I have come to you for help. Please help me and I swear to God that I will always be grateful to you and remain faithful in every way." Veer Singh responded.

Hakim sized up Veer Singh in one quick look and thought for a while. He was touched by Veer Singh's tenacity and was convinced that he could be a good worker for him. He, in fact, wanted to hire someone like him for his business and future travel plans.

Thus, Hakim decided to keep him, and this was the beginning of a new chapter of life for Veer Singh. Hakim asked his servant to get meals for Veer Singh and provided him a small room in his house. He asked Veer Singh to take a rest and have some sleep as he had not slept for quite some time.

Veer Singh was overwhelmed with emotions and wondered if it was a dream come true. He could not believe that Hakim would accept him give him a room to stay. He thanked God for His help.

When he woke up the next morning, he was fresh and full of excitement. He felt that his prayers had been miraculously answered. Hakim was a person who was going to be his mentor. Hakim had confided in him, and this was a great foundation for him. He was indebted to him for his kindness. He had Rs. 1000/- with him which he handed over to Hakim for safekeeping.

Hakim's family was very nice, and they treated him very well. Hakim was fond of eating different varieties of food. His cook would make different delicious dishes for him, and he was looked after well. Life was going on with high hopes and his mind was prepared to accept new challenges.

At night, he would remember his friends, mother, and relatives, wondering how they might have reacted to his being missing from the village. He missed his friends. He remembered how his mother used to tell him stories, looked after him, and prepared meals for him. This made him sad but then he consoled himself with the conviction that someday, they would be together, and he would take care of his mother and she would live a comfortable life. In his wishful thinking, he would imagine providing her all comforts in life. He was convinced she would forgive him for his actions.

Hakim got in touch with his friend, Bagha, who was at the village and told him about Veer Singh. He told him that Veer Singh was staying with him.

Bagha replied back quickly. He explained how things had changed overnight since Veer Singh had left. It was a very shocking detail. In his own words, "I am shocked to see how Veeru has left the house, running away with the money that had been given for his sister's marriage. Veeru's mother is so distressed that she has gone crazy. She has lost her senses. She has been hitting her head against walls and crying endlessly. If anyone comes to see her, she keeps asking, 'Is this my son Veeru? Has he come back?' The shock has been too much for her. It would be better if Veer Singh returned to the village otherwise, she is going to die."

Hakim, on reading this letter, was extremely sad. Veer Singh had not told him all this. Hakim understood that the young boy had run away from home with money entrusted to him to seek better life. The obsession for better life had prevailed over all ties and he knew that under the circumstances, Veer Singh would not like to return for fear of being chastised and shamed.

Hakim wrote a letter to Bagha stating that he should contact Veer Singh's relatives and ask them to come to Karachi and take the young boy with them.

He tried to convince Veer Singh to return to his village with the words, "I would advise you that the way things stand, you should go back to the village, apologize for what has happened and when things become normal, you can come back here but with their permission and your mother's consent. It is still not very late. You must reconcile with the situation that could become grave otherwise." He went on, "I have already communicated with your relatives to come to Karachi and they will take you back. I will explain to them that you should be forgiven, and all this was done on an emotional terrain," Hakim explained to him.

Veer Singh was troubled by these developments. He was in a dilemma, genuinely hurt and puzzled. He was left to take the toughest and most decisive action in life. Going back to the village would mean that he would never be able to come back. And he despaired that in the village, there was no future. It would be very difficult to face the people there and there was not the remotest possibility that anyone would justify his action. Already, there was a kind of disgrace attached to him and having to live with it in the village would be most frustrating.

Veer Singh told Hakim that it was very difficult for him, but that he respected Hakim very much and he would wait for his relatives to come to Karachi and then go with them. He wanted Hakim to explain the things to them in a convincing way that would ensure that Veer Singh wouldn't face humiliation from them. Hakim assured him that he would do this for him.

It was for sure that the confrontation with his relatives would be a major disaster though his mother may forgive him. But what would he do there once he was back in the village? He made up his mind that nothing would stop him from coming back to Karachi and it was his sentiment that to achieve something, he had to sacrifice in return. The price could be desertion of his family and close friends for good.

After a couple of days, Hakim received a letter from the village that Veer Singh's mother was very sick, and she wanted to see her son. She was on her death bed, and she would die in peace if Veer Singh was there beside her bed. At this point, he agreed to go back with the unwavering intent that he would return to Karachi.

The journey to the village from Karachi was very agonizing for Veer Singh. He kept on reflecting his past and future. He was aware that whatever he had done would not be tolerated by anyone and he would be treated with contempt. Fearful of a disagreement with his relations, he was in a state of complete dejection. A great remorse had struck his mind and Veer Singh felt dismayed & traumatized. There was a series of inconsistent thoughts coupled with guilt in his mind. He decided that he would not let his mother die because of his actions and would stay with her to take care of her and return to Karachi when things become better.

Finally, he reached the village witnessing the familiar roads, streets, and pools of dirty water. Everything just appeared the same. But there was a bigger shock awaiting him - an impending catastrophe. He found that his mother had already passed away and had been cremated in his absence.

Veer Singh was extremely shocked and remained motionless for a long time with tears rolling down incessantly. His uncle, Charan Singh, was already there, taking care of the proceedings for the final rites. Everyone in the village was talking about him and condemning him, holding him responsible for her death and he felt that his world had fallen apart.

The anguish and pain were too much for him. He cursed himself for this and was remorseful of what his decision had cost him. He was treated like a condemned person in the village with no one to share his sorrow and grief. He felt abandoned and banished from the society. There was no one in the village to listen to his feelings of remorse.

Realizing that he was not welcome in the village, Veer Singh decided to return to Karachi. This time there was no one to stop him. Moreover, he did not have any family member there, no brother, father, or mother. The village life did not have any future for him. He took a similar route to Karachi and returned to Hakim's house.

Travels & Future Events

On seeing him, Hakim consoled him and this made him feel easy. Battling with sorrow and grief, Veer Singh tried to reconcile himself with the situation. In a way, this turn of events gave him more strength to pursue future goals and face the reality.

Hakim had his own preconceived plans for Veer Singh. He felt that this young boy's emotions, helplessness, dependency, strengths, stamina, and sincerity could be used to his advantage. Being adventurous and obsessed with travelling and exploring different parts of world, Hakim Hashim Ali had been planning to visit Iran, China, Baluchistan, and Russia. He felt that Veer Singh would be an ideal attendant for these travel missions. He knew he would not have to pay anything to Veer Singh because he was loyal and obedient and obligated to him for taking him in.

He said to Veer Singh one day, "Look, I have plans to go to Iran, Russia, and Baluchistan and I want you to accompany me. You will gain a lot of experience in life. You will be with me all the time and will have the opportunity to meet many famous people. My previous trip to Alaska was a real challenge. It was extremely cold, and the weather was hard to beat but it was one of the loveliest places in the world. We will go there as a team. I have also invited Bagha to accompany us. He is very good in cooking. Both of you will enjoy this trip."

This was a very exciting proposal to Veer Singh. He instantly expressed his consent and started dreaming about the countries that he had seen only in maps.

Bagha was a cook by profession and was very good in making dishes which Hakim relished. Hakim always liked different cuisine and good food served in style. It fitted into his scheme of things. So, he asked Bagha to join them in their travel. Bagha was very devoted to Hakim, and he came to Karachi in a short time. The whole team was united.

While at Karachi, people belonging to the Buloch tribe would come to Hakim for treatment. Hakim was very popular with the Buloch people who happened to be of Iranian ethnicity. They were part of another Iranian ethnic group.

Baluchistan is an arid desert and mountainous region on the Iranian plateau in South-western Asia, northwest of the Arabian Sea. It stretches across South-western Pakistan, South-eastern Iran, and a small section of South-western Afghanistan. The southern part of Baluchistan is known by its historical name, Makran.

Baluchistan is named after the native Buloch tribes who inhabit the region and use Buloch as their native language. Persian, Pashtu, and Urdu are used as second languages.

During that time, it was ruled by four princely states: Makran, Kharan, Las Bela, and Karat. One part of Baluchistan is controlled by Afghanistan. The Baluchistan region is administratively divided among three countries, namely: Pakistan, Afghanistan, and Iran. The Pakistani portion of Baluchistan is the largest in area and its capital is the city of Quetta. Other major cities include Gwadar, Turbot, Khaddar, Sibiu, and Karat. Although Buloch nationalists have never accepted Baluchistan as a part of Iran, the governments of Pakistan and Iran insist on their sovereignty over parts of Baluchistan.

Hakim was very popular with the Baluchi people. He spoke their language and they considered him as their esteemed family doctor. They invited Hakim to Baluchistan to stay with them for some time. They desperately needed a doctor to look after their health-related issues.

Everything was set for the journey to Baluchistan, Iran, and Russia and Veer Singh was excited about his first big overseas adventure. This was the beginning of a challenge to explore the unobserved world.

The starting point of their journey was from Karachi, on a ship going to Pasny port, and from there it went to Cape Bakran. Hakim had two brothers working in the Iranian government and staying at Cape Bakran. They stayed there for a few days. His brothers treated them very well and they had one slave who would look after the guests. Besides a government official, Nazim was also deputed to look after them. The slave worked as a cook and would make excellent meat dishes from a freshly-slaughtered animal.

Veer Singh had the opportunity to see this city. He was quick in learning the language and was soon able to communicate fluently with the locals.

After some time, they boarded another ship, a white one named "St. Patrick". When they landed at a small town called "Gamo," they were greeted by a Buloch sardar by the name of Sayeed Khan. The sardar took them to his palace and after feeding them, he entered a discussion with Hakim about the problems that his people were facing.

He said to Hakim, "My people are very good, but they are addicted to opium, and I would appreciate it if you would suggest some measures to eradicate this evil. I am willing to pay any price for this."

Hakim had a lot of expertise in medicine so he assured Sardar that he would prepare a medicine for getting over this addiction. In a couple of days, he prepared a kind of oil to relieve this problem. The oil was good in taste and worked very effectively. This was his home-made medicine and people were experiencing positive effects from this. The sardar's brother who was an addict also benefitted from this medicine. The prescription, however, stipulated a standard dose of quinine which should not be exceeded.

Unfortunately, the sardar's brother was a careless person and would often forget to take the correct dose. At times, he missed the dose and at other times, he took more than what was required. On one such occasion, he drank an overdose of oil which started having an adverse reaction. He fell sick and his condition became critical. Everyone in the palace feared for his serious condition.

His aides immediately summoned Hakim and he started invasive treatment. He decided to give him an enema. Veer Singh was his attendant and he asked him to get some boiling water. He then asked the sardar's aides to take off his brother's pants so that he could commence his treatment. At this, his aides were infuriated and questioned how he could dare to ask their sardar's brother to take off his pants. They became so enraged that they threatened to kill Hakim.

Hakim was upset and so was Veer Singh. They sensed trouble and then Veer Singh told Hakim in Urdu that he would go and call the senior sardar who was the eldest in their family and explain the situation. Hakim agreed as that was the best thing to do under the circumstances.

Hakim told his aides that he was going to send Veer Singh to get some medicines and instead sent him to Sardar's palace where the latter was taking his meal.

The sardar, on hearing Veer Singh, was very upset about his brother's condition and immediately rushed to the scene. Hakim told the sardar that in case his brother did not get an enema, he could die. The sardar, on hearing this, lost his composure and said, "Well, if he dies, you also may have to die." Hakim was stunned to hear this and went pale with fear.

Eventually, Hakim successfully performed the operation and the sardar's younger brother recovered. The sardar was now very happy at this positive development, and he thanked all of them. They had a lavish meal together and Veer Singh enjoyed the sumptuous meal while conversing in Farsi.

The sardar was impressed by the eloquent use of Farsi by Veer Singh and wondered how Veer Singh could speak Farsi so well.

Veer Singh told him that he had learnt it from the Buloch people while travelling.

Hakim, being the impatient person, soon became bored and decided to move on. He told Sardar about his plans. As they were preparing for their next destination, the sardar told Hakim that he would like to extend help because they had done a wonderful job for his people and his brother in particular.

Sardar Sayeed Khan was Sunni Muslim, but his wife was Shia, a lady from a very prominent family of Iran. Sardar Sayeed Khan told Hakim that his wife would also be travelling to a certain place with guards, and they could accompany her and that it would be a safe journey for them. He arranged some soldiers and 18 guards with camels to accompany his wife and Hakim's party. The sardar also prepared an advance team that would make arrangements for food and the night stay. The party had 700 guns with them for their security.

During those days, the route of the journey on land was not safe; there were lots of bandits on the route. Afghan bandits would smuggle arms and sell them illegally to criminals. In those days, there were two major arms dealers — one French and one British. Both were authorized dealers for arms. They would buy arms and route them through Pakistan for sale to the Buloch people. The Buloch people whom they came across were considered honest and nice.

One evening, while they were camping, some 400 Afghan bandits appeared, and they surrounded the camp. The sardar's wife was staying in one camp whereas Hakim and his friends were staying in a different camp nearby. The Afghans presumed that Hakim was a British spy and started interrogating him. They took Hakim and Bagha to a different place. Veer Singh immediately went to the camp to contact the sardar's wife. She was a very tall & courageous lady. She came out of her camp and listened to what had happened. She immediately reached out to the Afghans and told them that Hakim was their family doctor who had also done good job for their community. They believed her and apologized leaving the place. Hakim got a lifeline.

Hakim was relieved and thanked Veer Singh for his sensible timely move. Finally, they had to part from the sardar's wife and proceeded on their own. They were given some shotguns and 5 rifles. Hakim had no knowledge of these weapons as he had never used them. He however would brag to everyone that he was expert in their use.

The journey was without any further incident and finally they reached the city of Tabas On, reaching the border of the city. The government officials confiscated all their guns on the grounds that they were illegal and gave them a receipt. They were asked to show proof of their legal purchase which they did and they continued their journey.

One afternoon, when Hakim was riding on a donkey, Veer Singh fell down and in the process, the gun that he was carrying fired. Luckily, no one was hurt. But Hakim was petrified. In due course they reached the city of Jiroft which is in the province of Kerman in Iran. It is located in vast plains surrounded by two rivers. It is one of the hottest places in the world and in 1933, the temperature soared to 55 degrees Celsius. There were mountains all over, presenting a very beautiful vision, however.

One incident that caused them some concern took place when Hakim, who was riding on a camel with a gun on his shoulders, suddenly disappeared, when the camel slipped and fell into a deep crater. Everyone was startled and all of them looked for Hakim. He was not to be seen anywhere. But to the surprise of all, Hakim was seen hanging on to the branches of a tree shouting, "Hey, I am here, please help me!" Bagha and Veer Singh pulled him, and he fell to the ground. Hakim had such a narrow escape that he remained in a state of shock for quite some time. The crater was so deep that nobody wanted to go there. The gun that he was carrying had slipped from Hakim's shoulders. They were all in a hurry to move on since there were tigers and other wild animals and dangerous insects all over the place.

They stayed at Jiroft for a few months. Hakim opened a temporary clinic, and it was very successful in a short time. Sardar Sayeed Fatehullah, the chief of the town, came to know about Hakim because his reputation had preceded him. He wanted to see if Hakim could look at his eye since he was facing some problems with it. He was confident that Hakim would be able to fix his eye problems. After examination, Hakim fixed the date for an operation.

Sardar Fatehullah was 6 feet tall, good-looking and very strong. He could eat one baby lamb all by himself in a single meal. He would often joke with Hakim saying that his people had spoiled his appetite. He said, in his own words, "Because you people don't eat much, I am always hungry in your company."

Hakim often bragged about being a good shot which he never was. He was unaware of the fact that Sardar Fatehullah was an excellent shot. The eye operation was successfully conducted, and he was asked to open his eyes. He told his grandson to bring his gun and he shot three bullets, each one striking over the other one. Then he asked Hakim to shoot and handed over the gun to Hakim.

Hakim was in a fix. He had never been good with guns, though he had always bragged about being a perfect shooter. And now this was the real test. Reluctantly, Hakim took the gun and aimed at the target, but his shot was 6 inches off the mark. Everyone was left laughing at Hakim who hid his face in embarrassment..

Later, Hakim started on to his next destination. Sardar Fatehullah, the city chief, accompanied them to Bam, a city in the province of Kerman. This city was famous for its exquisite clothes. One famous traveller wrote about this city:

"Over there, they weave excellent, beautiful, and long-lasting cotton cloths which are sent to places all over the world. There, they also make excellent clothes, each of which costs around 30 dinars."

Unfortunately, when they reached Bam with the sardar, the authorities arrested the sardar accusing him to be a robber. They took all his camels, horses, and even grand kids and he was taken away to another place. At this, Hakim and Veer Singh were very upset, but Sardar Fatehullah said to them, "Don't worry about this. This is part of our life and we have been into this kind of situation often. My people will take care of all this." After staying in Bam for a short time, the team moved to the city of Kerman.

Kerman is a big city in Iran. It is the centre of Kerman province. Located in a large and flat plain, this city is on the south of Tehran, capital of Iran.

At Kerman, they were guests of the Indian counsellor. He was British. The travellers noticed that the Iranian army did not have any uniform and they were wearing whatever they liked. They were often ridiculed by others, and they felt disgusted for not having a dress code.

During the time that they were in Kerman, Hakim started his practice and became popular very quickly. He had treated the Sardar earlier and this earned him a good reputation. A large of number of people wanted to get treatment from him and soon, he was making plenty of money. In just two months, he made 8 to 10 thousand dinars which was a substantial amount at that time. The mayor of Kerman also wanted to get treatment from Hakim and the travellers were invited to his house as guests. The Mayor treated them very well in his big house. After the meal, the Mayor also wanted to pay Hakim generously, but Hakim did not accept money from him and thanked him for his generous hospitality.

After some time, they moved to another town. The next destination was Mashhad. This is the second largest city in Iran. Sardar Fatehullah had arranged a caravan so that they could travel to Mashhad safely. The people running the caravan were deployed by the commissioner and were instructed to send a letter of confirmation from Hakim about safe arrival and they were to be paid 10/- rials each for this.

While travelling to Mashhad, a town called Rafsanjan was on the way. They stopped there for a while. Veer Singh who had two riyals asked some farmers to get them some pomegranates. On receiving two riyals, they brought two full bags on a donkey. Veer Singh told them politely that he did not want so much. It was beyond imagination that just two riyals could buy so much. In fact, it was a gift from those farmers to them. Curiously, they wanted to weigh the two bags. They were surprised to know that the bags weighed 9 pounds. Hakim paid them 10 riyals more which they reluctantly accepted and thanked him. Fruits are in abundance in Iran and also extremely cheap. They are of the highest quality in the world.

Finally, they reached Mashhad. Mashhad is one of the holiest cities in the Shia world, close to the borders of Afghanistan and Turkmenistan. They stayed in a caravan (sarai) which was not very comfortable for living. So, they changed the accommodation the next day. They did not plan to stay in Mashhad for long as they wanted to go to Russia. But to enter Russia, a passport was a requirement. Hakim asked someone to arrange three Iranian passports so that they could enter Russia. The person agreed to get three passports and would charge 20 riyals for each passport. During those days, a passport consisted of just a piece of paper without any photo. Anyone could travel on this piece of ID. Since India was ruled by the British, they did not like Indians to go to Russia. For this reason, they preferred to take Iranian passports.

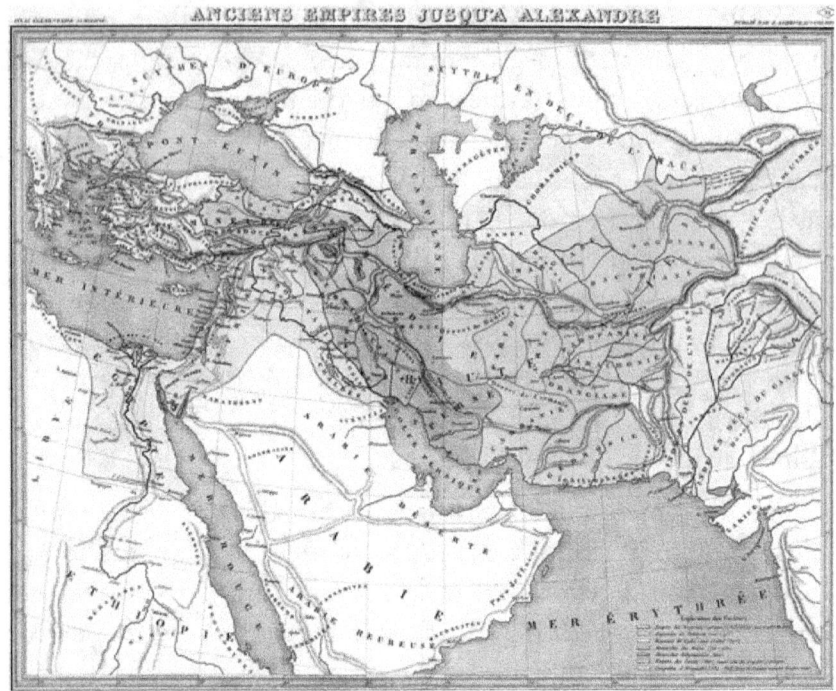

On procuring Iranian passports, they went to Baj Giran (on the border between Russia and Iran). From there, they moved to Dushanbe (now in Tajikistan). Hakim, who was carrying with him a set of books on medicines, had to make a list of them and declare them in a statement. They further moved to Ishadwad and then to Bukhara (now in Uzbekistan). They were travelling with donkeys and horses. At Bukhara, the government authorities again checked all their books and belongings. They stayed in an inn in Bukhara and converted all their money to gold. It was apparently due to currency problems. Before moving from Mashhad, they had already purchased heavy woolen jackets and overcoats in anticipation of extremely cold weather in Russia. Bukhara was under the control of Russia.

Hakim set up a clinic at Bukhara and soon people started flocking to him for treatment. Soon, the news reached the Amir of Bukhara. He was suffering from some sexual dysfunctional problems and wanted to be treated by Hakim. Hakim was called to see Amir and it was customary that anyone going to see Amir would have to wear clothes given by his aides. When Hakim entered the palace of Amir, there were soldiers all around for his security. Hakim was given velvet clothes to wear. The Amir of Bukhara maintained his sovereignty and Bukhara had its own currency. They also had a barter system. The whole city was very beautiful, and Veer Singh soon became well acquainted with the city. Hakim's treatment of the Amir of Bukhara was a great success, and Amir was greatly pleased with the former.

The Amir of Bukhara Mohammad, Alum Ali Khan

Everything was going very well for the three of them. One morning, while they were having breakfast, an officer arrived and told Hakim that his daughter was having severe pain and he would have to accompany him immediately. Hakim asked Veer Singh and Bagha to get his bags ready and when they reached his house, they were taken to an office instead. They started asking questions about their identity. Hakim was surprised. He said that he thought that he was there to see a patient. But they did not answer him. They were taken to another officer and all their possessions, including books were seized. Another person who spoke Farsi joined them. He assured them that everything would be fine. He was a government officer in disguise who wanted to extract information from them. They were taken to another room where they stayed overnight and were given a blanket with little food which was of very poor quality. This was a kind of lock up room.

Veer Singh was sickened by the sight of the food, and the way they were treating the prisoners. It was shocking. He got diarrhoea and did not eat anything. One of the guards noticed that Hakim and his friends had some money and he told them that they could get food from outside at their own expense. Next day, they were produced in the court and charged for having entered the country on fake Iranian passports. The officials decided that they would be deported to Iran. After a week, an official from the Indian counsellor's office came to see them. He spoke Farsi with them, but they did not trust him. Hakim admitted that they were Indians and were travelling on Iranian passports. The official told them that they would be deported to Iran where the Iranian government would be taking action on the issue of fake passports. There were 70 other persons who were also waiting to be deported to Iran. All these people were put in different groups.

When everything had been officially worked out for deportation, one official suddenly appeared and objected that these three people should not be deported. Hakim was taken aback because it meant that they would be kept in prison for more time. After a debate of one hour, it was agreed that they be sent to Iran. They were then taken to Ishadwad and placed in a camp. Here they were free to move within a designated area.

Amir of Bukhara

Another person who was an opium addict joined them. This person was always asking them for money to buy some opium. They were soon taken to Tashkent and there were many beautiful sights on the way. From there, they were moved to Mashhad and handed over to Iranian authorities. They spent the night in confinement and the next day, they were to be produced in court. This person who was an addict was an Iranian. On reaching Iran, he started threatening them. He demanded that they hand over all the money in their possession, otherwise, he would disclose their crime to the Iranian authorities who would seize all their money. Hakim wanted to compromise with him and was willing to give him some money, but he wanted all of their money.

Hakim offered him half the money, but the opium addict would not agree. There was an Armenian who was standing there listening to their arguments. He came to Hakim and asked him if he was an Indian. Hakim said yes, he was. Then he rose and got hold of this addict and started beating him up. He abused him and threatened to kill. The addict ran away, and this Armenian gentleman took them to his house. He was very kind to them, and he not only provided them meals but also washed their clothes. Hakim told him the entire story and the situation that they were placed in. He thought for a moment and said he would see what could be done to help them. He arranged horses for them, prepared legal papers for them, gave them four ashrafis (local currency in gold), and moved them from Mashhad to Amjelli, a town in the Caspian Sea area. He advised them what statement they should be giving to the authorities to cover up the issue.

The officials were satisfied with Hakim's statement and allowed them to go. From Pahlavi, they boarded a ship and reached the British Counsellor's office in Russia. From the counsellor's office they sent a cable to Hakim's brother in Karachi informing him about their predicament. They stayed at the British counsellor's office in Rashad for 21 days. After that, the Russian government officials received orders not to send them to Iran. They were allowed to stay in Russia and if required, be sent to India instead of Iran so that they may not get robbed again.

Veer Singh narrated an interesting anecdote about his experiences in Russia. While they were staying in Russia with the British counsellor who was a Jew, they came across his servant who was totally uneducated but had devised a clever mathematical system that was unique. He could keep accounts of every item purchased by him up to six months without putting anything in writing. He was offered 500/- to disclose this unique method, which was a substantial amount of money then, but he did not agree to disclose this art.

In the process of going back to India, they went to Peharabi and from there to Bet Qbek, a seaport. They were travelling in a ship. In the morning, Veer Singh was hungry as he had not eaten for two days. When he found something packed in a gunny bag, he wanted to take it out.

The captain of the ship noticed it and he sent the message not to do so. Veer Singh told him that he had not eaten for days and as such, was tempted to have something to eat. Upon hearing this, the captain invited him and his friends for breakfast, and they had coffee and biscuits. Next morning, they reached Bet Qbek. That was the end of their journey on the ship. From there, they got on the train to Batoon, an oil port in Turkey. There was snow all over. From there they went to Istanbul via Traboodan. At Istanbul, they went to stay in an area which was mainly inhibited by Iranians. At that time, 1911, Mohammad Ali Shah Qatar was Khalifa of Turkey. From there, they went to Isnaqeer (Turkey) and then to Port Suez (Egypt). Suez is a way station for pilgrims travelling to and from Mecca. They changed ships and boarded an Italian ship and this journey lasted 8 days. They went to Beirut and remained there for a couple of hours. From there, they returned to Bombay through the Dardania passage.

Hakim and his friends were relieved to be in India, their own country. They did not have any money, not even the fare to travel to Karachi. They were completely broke. They stayed in Musafirkhana, a free inn. In the morning, they went out for breakfast. It was an Iranian restaurant owned by Mohammad Sadegh who owned three more restaurants in the town. Hakim and Bagha returned to the Musafirkhana to take rest while Veer Singh stayed at the restaurant.

Veer Singh could speak Farsi well and was quite eloquent in the language. He started a conversation with others in Farsi who were surprised to see his fluency in the language.

He asked the waiters if he could get a job there and one of the waiters suggested that he should see Mohammad Sadegh who owned the restaurant. He waited for Mohammad Sadegh for hours and finally when he came to the restaurant, he enquired if he could get a job.

Mohammad Sadegh, a very tall person, looked at him and sized him up. He was impressed by Veer Singh's conversation and his fluency in both Farsi & Urdu.

"How did you learn Farsi? You speak very well, and it is quite surprising to me because it is not common here," asked Mohammad Sadegh.

"Well, I was in Baluchistan for quite some time. I was there with many friends, and I was keen to learn the language," Veer Singh replied.

This seemed unusual to Mohammad Sadegh, and he realized that Veer Singh could be a good worker for his restaurant, not only because of his conversational skill, but also because he was intelligent and appeared trustworthy. He decided to give him the job.

The purpose of getting this job was to earn some money so that he could go back to Karachi with Hakim. He wanted to raise one hundred rupees, enough for the train fare from Bombay to Karachi for three persons.

Mohammad Sadegh was looking for a person who could assist him with responsibilities in handling the restaurant business with honesty. He could sense that this young person had the required capabilities. He took him inside the work area where food was being prepared. In four days, Veer Singh had practically learned everything and was ready to work independently. After completing the required training, he started working on his own and took up responsible assignments.

The next day, he told Mohammad Sadegh that he wanted to borrow one hundred rupees as a loan as he had some friends who were staying in the inn and had to go back to Karachi. Mohammad Sadegh gave him one hundred rupees instantly and Veer Singh thanked him.

"I will give this money to my friends who are staying at the inn and come back. If you want, you can send someone with me to make sure that I am not running away with this borrowed money," Veer Singh explained.

"If you intend to leave me by taking this money, I am afraid this is not going to be enough. You should take some more money." Mohammad Sadegh exclaimed.

"No sir, I just need this money to help my friends and I promise that I will work with honesty. I thank you very much for this support."

He went to the Musafirkhana to give the money to Hakim and Bagha. Hakim promised to return the money on his arrival at Karachi and it was agreed that Veer Singh would join them after saving some money from his job at the restaurant.

Veer Singh started working for Mohammad Sadegh and soon his business was growing, and he was entrusted with more responsibilities — collecting money, making purchases, pay rolls, workers accounts, and marketing. He had to supervise all his restaurants. Mohammad Sadegh was satisfied that his restaurants were in safe hands, and he could concentrate on other activities. Besides restaurants, he had a bakery shop, a flour mill and was considered a prominent figure among the Iranian community. He was originally from Yazd, Iran. Now, Veer Singh was running the business for him.

But deep down in his heart, he still wanted to be with Hakim and Bagha. He was planning to save some money so that he could leave this job and once again join his friends. He was waiting to receive money that Hakim had promised to send him and often enquired from Mohammad Sadegh if Hakim had sent some money for him. But Sadegh Mohammad told him that he had not received anything from Hakim.

Veer Singh got dismayed and wondered how his close friends could turn away from their promise to return the money. Every day, he would enquire from Mohammad Sadegh and got upset when he said "no". It was beyond his imagination.

Finally, Mohammad Sadegh disclosed to Veer Singh that Hakim had sent some money long time back, but he intentionally did not tell him because he did not want to lose him. "I want you to stay with me and you will have a bright future here. Let us work together and create a better tomorrow. I treat you like my son, and I don't want to lose you. My fear was that you might leave me to join your friends. You must trust me," Mohammad Sadegh said to him.

It was true that Mohammad Sadegh was treating him like a family member and took good care of him. Wherever he was with him, he always introduced him as his son in public. In return, Veer Singh never took any money for his long hours of work. He liked to wear good clothes and Mohammad Sadegh knew it and always provided him with them. Other than this, he never sought any luxuries and devotion to work was his passion. He looked after his business well and it was expanding.

During this period, he got converted to Islam. He was given the name Gholam Hussein. He took control of the business and was making decisions on his own. Mohammad Sadegh was entirely satisfied to see his business growing. He spent his time in other businesses and personal activities and left everything to Gholam Hussein Paksima to decide. He continued working for Mohammad Sadegh for 11 years and during this tenure, he never took any money for personal use. It was like a voluntary service in a family business. He was always in touch with his friends but did not get any opportunity to meet them.

During this period, Mohammad Ali Shah, the King of Iran, abolished the constitution because he felt it was not according to

Islamic laws. He bombarded the parliament with the help of the army and support from Russia and Britain.

Faced by the prospect of an imminent revolution within the country, Mohammad Ali Shah, the king, was forced to flee to Russia. Later on, he took refuge in Constantinople and died there. Gholam Hussein was quite disturbed by these developments.

Gholam Hussein Paksima had to devote much time for the business and there was no relief, no holiday, vacation or any other entertainment. He had to convert coins to paper currency and had to pay one anna extra for one rupee paper note. The restaurants were doing good business and there was cash flow of three to four thousand rupees per day. By today's standards, it would amount to 180,000 to 240,000 rupees per day. It was obvious that running a business of this level would have put tremendous pressure on him.

Clash of Principles

Once during his routine inspection, he found that one worker who was his long-time employee, had been misusing plenty of wood for making wine at home. He was a hardworking and sincere worker and when asked why he was doing this, he confessed that he was burning the stolen wood to make wine. He was forced to do this because he could not afford to buy wood with the meager salary that he was getting. Gholam Hussein Paksima sympathised with this man because he was very hardworking and had been serving them for a long time. Being compassionate in nature, he wanted to help the worker. He made calculations and concluded that if this worker were paid a little extra, but not allowed to take away the wood, it would benefit more than it was losing wood. So, he told him that he would be paid extra but he would not be allowed to take away the wood. This arrangement was made to benefit the company according to his calculations.

After few months, Gholam Hussein was deputed to go out of town for some purchases and Mohammad Sadegh was taking care of the business himself after a long time. While making the payments to the workers, the same worker objected and demanded more money explaining that Gholam Hussein had agreed to pay extra allowance besides payroll. Mohammad Sadegh was puzzled but he paid him extra money anyway. He did not want to indulge in controversy and decided to discuss it with Gholam Hussein later.

In fact, Mohammad Sadegh had not been making decisions for the last 11 years and it was up to Gholam Hussein to handle the business and decided whatever seemed appropriate.

Mohammad Sadegh asked Gholam Hussein about this arrangement which he felt was contrary to his business policies.

"I don't understand why you made this arrangement of paying extra allowance. It is going to discourage other workers and will amount to favouritism and discrimination. Besides, if this person was taking away wood without your consent, you should have reprimanded him rather than increasing his pay with extra allowances. This sets up a bad precedent," Sadegh spoke while discussing with Gholam Hussein.

"I had made all the calculations before arriving at this decision. In fact, this worker has been very good at work and has served the company for a considerable time. He deserved a raise. It was fair that he is given a raise and advised not to take away wood anymore. In my view, giving him a little raise was appropriate as the cost of wood taken away by him amounts to more than a meager raise." Gholam Hussein explained.

"I decided to give him extra allowance in addition to his wages and if this was included in the wages, it would have been objectionable to others and caused resentment," Gholam Hussein further explained.

But Mohammad Sadegh was not convinced. He was a typical businessman and he felt very strongly that the worker should have been sacked for pilferage. He had no sympathy and did not understand the hardships of others. This can be seen from the fact that Gholam Hussein was never paid for 11 years and in all fairness, he should have had an account to his name wherein his monthly allowance should have been credited. But he never did so, and it is fair to assume that it was his selfish nature and greed for money that prevailed over his compassion for others. He told Gholam Hussein that this was sheer wastage of money and he was against his decision.

"My son, you don't take decisions in a wise manner. You don't realize the value of money. Do you know the value of one anna? I don't think you know how many annas there are in one rupee?

You have taken everything for granted!" Mohammad Sadegh said in a fit of frenzy.

Gholam Hussein had never expected this and was shocked at the attitude of his master whom he had treated like a father and for whom he had sacrificed 11 years of his youth. Mohammad Sadegh had clearly revealed his true nature as one that was filled with greed and selfishness coupled with ruthlessness.

Gholam Hussein was deeply hurt by this treatment. He had spent years of sleepless nights, working hard to grow the business, taking no personal money. He had sacrificed his youth for this business and had got nothing in return. He did not even go to see his friends he had been longing to see. After years of hard work, he did not have a single rupee in his pocket. It was beyond his imagination that Mohammad Sadegh, whom he considered his father, could treat him like this. He could have made lot of money if he had wanted to but he had sacrificed everything, every comfort with utmost honesty. Now Mohammad Sadegh was teaching him business techniques, telling him the value of one anna? While forgetting the millions he had made through the efforts of Gholam Hussein whom he called his son everywhere in society, Mohammad Sadegh had branded him as reckless, immature, and an extravagant person who meant nothing to him but a tool to exploit.

Gholam Hussein had always been compliant and submissive to his father. He always obeyed the decisions of Mohammad Sadegh. He did not want any further argument with him.

He said, "I have been handling thousands of rupees every day with utmost honesty. I have always given my best to the business and never took any money for personal use except buying clothes to wear. I did what was best for growth of business and tried to save every paisa by working day and night. Your business has grown in proportions over the years and still you say I do not know the value of money. After 11 years of my association with you, you still call me irresponsible and reckless? Alright, I say goodbye and must go out to find out how many annas there are in one rupee. I am leaving in one week." Gholam said this after much deliberation.

Mohammad Sadegh had never anticipated this. He was stunned but he was unmoved. He knew his Gholam Hussein too well. He was aware that once Gholam Hussein had made up his mind about something, there was nothing that could change him. He did not say a word.

He hoped that maybe he would change his mind after some thought.

But Gholam Hussein was deeply shocked and determined to leave. Soon the news spread in the company. He would not see things differently despite much persuasion by Ali Gomi, a senior employee in the restaurant. Mohammad Sadegh gave him rupees 50/- for his journey and he purchased some biscuits and fruits and after paying for the ticket, he was left with just 14/- rupees. Mohammad Sadegh did not acknowledge that after years of hard work, Gholam Hussein deserved a much bigger package and giving rupee 50/- was a kind of cruel joke.

Gholam Hussein Paksima left for Karachi the next morning to meet his old friends. In the train, he thought over the time he had spent in the company owned by Sadegh Mohammad and how it ended up without any remuneration. He thought about how the world could be so cruel with human beings devoid of any feelings of compassion and love. What was the significance of relationships? How could people betray each other in their greed for money? He had given everything to Mohammad Sadegh but in return he was treated like an outsider.

After reaching Karachi, he went to see Hakim. Hakim was now a thoroughly changed person. Gholam Hussein told him his story and requested him to return Rs. 1000/- which he had deposited with him. Hakim refused to give him the money saying that he had done many favours to him and taken him to many countries which involved a lot of money, and he had no right to claim the money.

Still Gholam Hussein did not argue with him. He parted with good relations without any ill feeling and did not utter a word of displeasure to Hakim. Hakim told him that during his next journey, he would like to be accompanied. However, Gholam Hussein's hopes had been dashed to the ground.

His whole world had crumbled but he did not lose courage. Life had given him many bitter lessons and he had become mature by virtue of his experiences. Life had given him very turbulent times, but he would not give up and continue with time to move on. Travelling with Hakim and working at Mohammad Sadegh's company had made him strong. He had faced many tough times and this moment in his life could not deprive him of his positive outlook towards life. He was prepared to face the challenges of life boldly and thus started making plans.

The Pains of Progress

Gholam Hussein Paksima started looking for a job to make a fresh start. He had no money with him and had not eaten anything. He was staying in a Musafirkhana. In search of a job, he wandered all around the city, but getting a job was not easy. One of the reasons for not getting the job was his expensive dress style. He always wore fancy clothes with a gold ring and appeared to be rather well off. Most people did not believe that he was seriously looking for a job.

While getting a job was not easy, he had no money in his pocket; he would have just one square meal in a day. He was starving and had not eaten for three days. Then he met one maulana named Taj Mohammad in the court building where he was doing odd legal jobs like preparing documents. The maulana was eating food and there was a matka (a pitcher) of water. Having not eaten anything for the last three days, his physical condition was very bad. He asked Maulana if he could get some water. The maulana responded favourably and when he took a sip of the water on an empty stomach, he fell on the ground and became unconscious.

The maulana immediately got up and sprinkled some water on his face. He sensed that he had not eaten anything and when he regained his senses, he offered him tea with some snacks. Then he asked him if he needed some help.

Gholam Hussein told him that he was looking for a job. The maulana told him that with these fancy clothes, no one would offer him a job. He presumed that he had run away from home. The maulana said that if this was the case, he would write a letter to his family members so that they could come over and take him back home.

Gholam Hussein told him his entire story, but the maulana did not believe him. Gholam Hussein told him that his parents were dead, and he was all alone.

Maulana said to him "I have a job, but it is a very low paid job, and it will be hard to make a living on it. It is a tough job with long hours."

"Will I be able to have meals two times a day?" Gholam Hussein asked curiously.

"Yes, it is just rupee 10 per month."

"Who was doing this job before? If a human being was doing this job, I also can do it!" Gholam Hussein was optimistic.

He accepted the offer and the maulana suggested that they could visit the job site in the evening.

Later in the evening, they took a tram from the courthouse that took them to Parsi Bazaar. The Maulana took him to the second floor of an old-fashioned building. Gholam Hussein was puzzled initially and finally they arrived at a hall called the Public Library. It was a hall with books and magazines all around. The maulana told him that the library would be open to the public from 4.00 PM to 10.00 PM and in the morning, he would have to clean the floor, chairs and tables, arrange the books, and keep an account of the customers. He would also be responsible for the membership fee collections. There was a small room attached to the hall that had a washroom as well. The maulana suggested that he stay in that small room.

The maulana described the library norms to Gholam Hussein. He told him that the library was being run by the Zia Ul Islam society and that the membership fee was four annas per month. Unfortunately, most of the people infringed on their payments. It would be his responsibility to recover the outstanding dues.

While Maulana kept on talking about the library, the people, and the social problems, Gholam Hussein was very hungry and wanted to eat something. Then, finally the maulana gave him the keys and was about to go. Unable to hold himself, Gholam

Hussein said to him, "I have to ask you for a favour. In fact, I have given my clothes for washing and have to collect them. I just need one rupee so that I can collect them." The maulana gave him one rupee and left. Gholam Hussein immediately went to a dhaba (a restaurant) where he had some food that gave him some strength to go on.

After coming back to his room, he wondered how much money he was going to need to survive on a salary of ten rupees a month. That was just 30 paisa a day. He calculated that with this money, he could have just one meal and some tea in the morning. Tea was for one paisa, bread for two paisa, and lunch would cost him 5 paisa. He decided that he would take tea with some bread in the morning, skip lunch and have a meal in the evening.

To start with, he purchased two kilos of baked chana (grams) so that he could eat when there was nothing else to eat.

The maulana continued to be sceptical about Gholam Hussein's past life. He did not believe his story. He hoped that someday he would tell him the real story.

Gholam Hussein, while going through the library records, found that there were many defaulters who had not paid their dues for a long time. He started collecting outstanding dues and convinced the people about the benefits of the library and its continued operation. Eventually, the entire outstanding amount was collected and the maulana was very happy with the progress Gholam Hussein had made. His salary was raised to 15/- rupees per month. The chairman of the library, a prominent citizen, was Sir Abdullah Haroon and he took note of the progress of the library. He was national leader of the Muslim League. Haroon had been a member of the Karachi municipality since May 1913. He was active in social welfare projects throughout his life. He liked Gholam Hussein personally and recommended a raise in his salary to rupee 100 per month. This was due to the fact that he had undertaken more than his share of responsibilities and had improved the service offered by the library. The membership base had increased substantially.

Gholam Hussein took this opportunity to improve his English and he kept on reading books to gain knowledge in various fields that interested him.

Through his communication with Hakim, he came to know that Hakim had moved to Iran. He wrote to him about his present job and his desire to visit Iran for better opportunities. He told him that his job at the library was satisfactory, but he would not be able to progress in life on the basis of this job.

Hakim wrote back to him telling him that he would help him to settle down in Iran and with his hard work, he would have a better position in life.

Encouraged by Hakim's words, Gholam Hussein quit the job and went to Iran where he met Hakim. He was happy to have him back and started looking for a job for Gholam Hussein.

Sir Abdullah Haroon
Prominent politician and philanthropist (1872 – 1942)

Hakim managed to get Gholam Hussein the job of a tally clerk on a ship with the Gray Paul Company which later became the Grey Mackenzie Company. His monthly pay would be 150/- per month. He remained in this company for couple of years and moved to different locations and eventually became superintendent in the company. He was disturbed over the Iran revolution. Being fond of poetry, he read it in the evening whenever he got some free time. His favourite poet was Ameer Parveen – an Iranian poet.

At the ship, he had to work on all three shifts. Sheikh Ali Majeed who was in charge of the Muslim League shared a room with him. He was making 300 to 400 rupees a week. In their free time, they discussed about the revolution in Iran quite often.

In those days, there was a crime syndicate run by a gangster. This gangster was making lot of money through illegal activities. They also worked in the ship, stealing merchandise belonging to company. They found that Gholam Hussein was an obstacle to their illegal activities as he was constantly watching them. They persuaded him to join them or face the consequences. Fearing that they could kill, Gholam Hussein reluctantly agreed to remain silent but would be no part of them. But they still considered him a threat and started making plans to get rid of him. One of the gang members tried to implicate Gholam Hussein with a planned conspiracy by keeping smuggled goods in his room and reporting it to the authorities. But Gholam Hussein apprehended the trouble and before they could report it to the authorities, he put all the merchandise back to the store and when his room was raided by authorities, there was nothing they could find. The vicious plan of his adversaries was foiled.

He realized that the environment was not good, and he could be falsely implicated anytime by his opponents. He therefore quit the job and went back to Bombay. In the train, he became very sick and when he reached Bombay, he was taken to a hospital. The hospital authorities asked for the address of his relatives and he said that he knew Mohammad Sadegh. They informed

Mohammad Sadegh about his illness who immediately rushed to the hospital and took care of him. Mohammad Sadegh's friend, Hassan Ramazan, too was there and he looked after Gholam Hussein.

When Gholam was fit to leave the hospital, Mohammad Sadegh took him to his house and in a couple of days, he was cured. Mohammad Sadegh told him that he was very sorry for what had happened earlier and admitted his mistake. He said to him that he would not allow him to leave again and offered him managerial position as before.

Once again, life started moving the same way, looking after restaurants, keeping accounts, purchases, and dealing with customers, officials and workers.

Mohammad Sadegh had some friends in Rangoon and they were planning to open up a restaurant there but did not have any experience in this field. They requested him to visit Rangoon and set up a restaurant for them. But Mohammad Sadegh was aware that his friends were also involved in illegal businesses and had a bad reputation in the town. Nevertheless, his friends insisted that he visit Rangoon and help them with the business. He agreed on one condition that there will be no illegal activity and either he or his son Gholam Hussein would stay with them for a period of one year. They agreed to this.

Mohammad Sadegh told Gholam Hussein about this plan. It was decided that Mohammad Sadegh would go to Rangoon first and make the initial setup required for the restaurant. In a fortnight, Mohammad Sadegh moved to Rangoon and started working on the set up of a restaurant for his friends.

Gholam Hussein stayed behind, managing usual activities and at the same time getting ready to move to Rangoon for another challenging opportunity with unknown partners.

The Rangoon Episode

A month after Mohammad Sadegh had left, Gholam Hussein received a letter from him asking him to come to Rangoon (now known as Myanmar) and bring some of things that he wanted there. He packed up and moved over there. In fact, he wanted to stay with Mohammad Sadegh but he had to be in agreement with his plans. Mohammad Sadegh advised him to stay there for one year and thereafter he would return to his home. He did not like the people over there, but he would abide by the wish of his father.

After leaving Gholam Hussein in Rangoon, Mohammad Sadegh returned to Bombay and started his customary business activities. Gholam Hussein continued to stay at Rangoon and the restaurant business started thriving. His assignment of one year to work with other people was completed and he opened a restaurant of his own in the same locality. This was not acceptable to the people he worked with, and they complained to Mohammad Sadegh.

Gholam Hussein explained to Mohammad Sadegh that his term to work for those people was over and now he had his own option. Further, he was not happy working with them anymore. Those people had continued with their criminal activities, and it was risky working with them. After long arguments, he had preferred to stay away from such people and opened his own restaurant.

Mohammad Sadegh was upset over this. He had a long conversation with his friends and they agreed that Gholam Hussein had the right to make his choice and they had nothing against him but they wanted Gholam Hussein to be part of their team.

Mohammad Sadegh, however, sensed that Gholam Hussein could be in trouble because he had chosen to leave them. They could go to any extent to harm him as they were involved in illegal activities. He told them that Gholam Hussein had separated because of their unlawful activities. At this, they were furious and they exchanged harsh words. Mohammad Sadegh was upset on hearing their allegations.

He immediately sent a message to Gholam Hussein asking him to wind up the business, close the restaurant, and return to Bombay as quickly as he could. Gholam Hussein complied and returned to Bombay after closing the business. It was in the year 1924 or 1925.

After some time, Mohammad Sadegh fell sick and died in Bombay. Gholam Hussein was in deep shock, and he felt as if his whole world had once again shattered. He spent days in anguish and sorrow. Once again, he had lost someone very close to him, one who had been like a father to him.

Gholam Hussein was in isolation. He felt lonely and did not like to work in the restaurants without his father figure – Mohammad Sadegh. The whole place seemed so isolated to him. He started smoking cigarettes.

Gholam Hussein decided to go to Yazd, Mohammad Sadegh's hometown for a change. He had a close friend named Syeed Bagher who was planning to see his family in Mashad. They discussed plans to make a visit to Mashad first and see the holy shrine of Imam Hussein and then Gholam Hussein could visit Yazd later.

On reaching Mashad, Sayeed Bagher invited Gholam Hussein to meet his wife's family and he enjoyed their company. They were very kind and friendly and Sayeed Bather's first-born, little Agha Reza, was a very cute baby. He realised that it time for him to get married. His friend Bather's wife had a younger sister and

Gholam Hussein asked for her hand in marriage and soon they were married. His wife's name was Fatemah. They got married at Mashad in the year 1926. Soon they had a beautiful daughter who was named Nusrat Khanum. After some time, they had a son who was named Kazem Agha.

He decided to stay at Mashad and set up a business with his brother-in-law, Mohammad Jaffer, who was a very pious person. He was taking care of his 3 sisters and mother. Life was going on well and the business with his brother-in-law, Mohammad Jaffer, was progressing well. They called him "Agha Daiee." However, the political scenario in Iran was changing. Mohammad Ali had fled from Iran and people had new constitution. Reza Shah was the new ruler and he wanted everyone to be registered and get a family Shenasnameh. So, Gholam Hussein and his brother "Agha Daiee" decided to go to get it done. There he selected the name "Paksima" and Agha Daiee said he also wanted the same. That is why cousins in Mashad have the same last name.

The Revolution in Iran

The cause of revolution - why the Shah (Mohammad Reza Pahlavi) was overthrown and why he was replaced by an Islamic Republic — is a subject of historical debate. The revolution was in part a conservative backlash against the westernization and secularization efforts of the western backed Shah. The Shah was perceived by many Iranians as a puppet of a non-Muslim western power (USA) whose culture was contaminating that of Iran. The Shah's regime was seen as oppressive, brutal, corrupt, and extravagant; it also suffered from basic functional failures — an overly-ambitious economic program that brought economic bottlenecks, shortages, and inflation. The founder of the dynasty, Army General Reza Pahlavi, replaced Islamic rule with western ones, and forbade traditional Islamic clothing, separation of the sexes, and veiling of women and the wearing of a hijab. Women who resisted his ban on wearing the hijab in public had their chadors (black garment covering almost all of head) forcibly removed and torn. In 1935, a rebellion by a pious Shia at the shrine of Imam Reza in Mashhad was crushed on his orders with dozens killed and hundreds injured, rupturing relations between the Shah and pious Shia in Iran.

The political situation in Iran was very disturbing and he had to face a lot of unpleasant situations. Somehow, Gholam Hussein Paksima continued to control the business with Agha Daiee but the government policy predominantly controlled by the British did not allow him to work in a business-friendly manner. Looking at the turn of events in Iran, Gholam Hussein Paksima decided to return to India with his family. Sayeed Bagher also travelled to Bombay, India with his family.

Family Tree

As mentioned earlier, Gholam Hussein got married to Fatemah in 1926 at Mashhad, Iran. Seven children were born to them. They were named as:

- Nusrat   -   Born on April 28, 1927 (Expired Aug 28, 1991)
- Kazem   -   Born on Jan 21, 1928
- Ali   -   Born on Dec 14, 1934
- Esmat   -   Born on July 24, 1937
- Mahmood   -   Born in Sep. 1938
- Ahmad   -   Born on April 1, 1940
- Talat (Sima)   -   Born on May 11, 1941

The name of Gholam Hussein's second wife was Sadigeh Mossaver and they were married in Mashad city in 1942. Seven children were born to them and their names are listed below.

- Tahira   -   Born in Mashad
- Razia   -   Born in Poona
- Mohammad Reza   -   Born in Mashad
- Zeenat   -   Born in Karachi
- Abbas   -   Born in Karachi
- Ali Raza   -   Born in Karachi
- Zaidoon   -   Born in Karachi

In 1930, when Gholam Hussein returned to Bombay, he started a restaurant in partnership with an Anglo Indian marine officer named James. It was named "Café Chevalier." He renovated the whole building and business picked up well. He continued with this business for several years.

James, his partner, was always shabbily dressed. In contrast to it, Gholam Hussein was always well dressed, and it was quite imperative for the business. Gholam Hussein advised his partner several times to dress properly so that his shabby dress did not cast a negative impression on the customers, but he never listened.

One day, Gholam Hussein was attending to some important customers when his partner came in, dressed rather shabbily. He asked him to stay away but his partner started talking rudely and they had an argument. Later, Gholam Hussein told him that if he continued like this, he would have to leave. But this man refused to compromise and instead Gholam Hussein had been served a notice. The matter went to the court and his partner James took control of the restaurant and spent all the money from the account of the restaurant whereas Gholam Hussein had to pay the legal expenses from his own pocket.

In 1942, he opened up a restaurant named "Coffee Club" in Bombay at Flora Fountain and purchased a house just behind the restaurant. There was a famous hotel named Watson Hotel which catered to whites only. It was located at a building named "Esplanade Mansion." The hotel was famous for its luxurious style, catering only to English people.

Gholam Hussein opened this restaurant named Coffee Club where he was the sole proprietor. The restaurant soon picked up sales and customers were very happy with good service. It was always full of customers at any given time. He continued in this restaurant business till 1945.

Fearing the impact of World War II in India, Gholam Hussein sent his wife and children - Nusrat, Kazem, Ali, Esmat, Mahmood, Ahmad, and Sima (who was a few months old) - to Mashad where his wife got pneumonia and despite getting the best treatment, passed away. She had been there for just 40 days. He got a telegram and managed to get a ticket to Mashad and planned to proceed by train from Delhi to Zehadan and from there to Mashad by car. At Delhi, he boarded the train to Zahedan. When he reached Sukker he was told that a major bridge had collapsed due to floods and that the railway traffic had been suspended. The army had taken over the movement and the few small boats were being primarily used to ferry troops and supplies. Gholam Hussein approached the officer in charge, explaining his urgency. The officer in charge was General Wavell. On seeing Gholam, he asked him, "What are you doing here?"

He ordered that a special boat be used to transport Gholam to the other side of the river. He managed to board a train to Zahedan via Quetta and finally he arrived at Mashad and came to know that his wife had already expired. He was shocked and decided that he would return to Bombay, sell Coffee Club, and do some other business.

His restaurant in Bombay "Coffee Club" was doing very well and soon more people had to be hired. It was his expertise in the field that helped the business to grow. In a short time, it became the most luxurious and famous restaurant in the state. Gholam Hussein soon became one of the prominent figures in the town. Looking for expansion, he saw an opportunity which he did not want to miss.

There was a famous Italian restaurant in Poona named E-Muratore. The restaurant was big; it had 100 waiters, 10 assistant managers, an orchestra, a bar, and a dance floor. The whole restaurant had a marble floor that was imported from Italy. It had a very exquisite look and catered to foreigners, rich and upscale customers. He sold his restaurant Coffee Club in Bombay and purchased the E-Muratore restaurant in Poona. The restaurant had an average turnover of Rs. 10000 to 15000 per day, which was substantial in those days.

Purchase of the Village of Fatehabad

In terms of Gholam Hussein's achievements and his ambitious plans to establish business, there was another business enterprise which he pursued very meticulously. The purchase of a village named Fatehabad in Mashad district is distinctive of his adventurous investment.

It happened after the death of his wife and having sold the Coffee Club, he planned to visit the native village Khosa Pando in Moga with his son Kazem. After his visit to the village, he returned to Mashad to look after his children and settled down there and started looking for further business opportunities. After taking into consideration various proposals and discussions with his sons, he decided to buy a village named Fatehabad, located about 40 kilometres south of Mashad. It was about 4km by 6km in area.

It is important to understand the rationale behind this move and it is therefore reasonable to understand the circumstances that were prevailing at this time because of World War II.

During the Second World War, the German army had pushed forward into Russia and were almost at the doorstep of Moscow. The King of Iran, Reza Shah, had a great affinity for the Germans and thus it was not surprising to see that they were active in Iran. Reza Shah had brought in many important developments in the country which included building infrastructure, expanding cities, transportation networks, and establishing schools. He also set forth on a policy of neutrality, but to help finance and support his ambitious modernization projects, he needed the help of the West. Germany considered Iran a very strategic partner because of oil.

For many decades, Iran and the German Empire had cultivated close ties, partly as a counter to the imperial ambitions of Britain and Russia, and later, the Soviet Union. Trading with Germany appealed to Iran because the Germans did not have a history of imperialism in the region, unlike the British and Russians. However, the British Empire and Soviet Union wanted Iran to be on their side and in the process, they invaded Iran. Although Iran had developed military strength, eventually the allies proved superior, and they defeated Iran on many fronts. The invading allies had 200,000 troops and modern aircraft, tanks, and artillery. British and American troops invaded Iran from the south and occupied Tehran, the capital of Iran; the Russians invaded Iran from the north and captured the northern provinces of Iran, all the way to Karaj. Mashad, being in the north, came under Russian occupation. Reza Shah was deposed and sent out of country to Bombay. Rumours were that he would be held in Bombay. However, the plans changed, and he was sent to exile as a British prisoner in South Africa where he died in 1944. His son, Mohammad Reza Shah, became the Shah of Iran.

Mr. Kazem narrates his experiences in going through all these difficult times. He and his Dad, Gholam Hussein, with a couple of brokers drove to Fatehabad and had to pass through Russian check posts. They passed the tomb of Firdausi, the epic poet of Iran, and paid homage to him. Finally, they reached Fatehabad. The village had a population of 300 households (mainly farmers) and covered a large piece of land.

Mr. Kazem narrates that on their way to Fatehabad, they saw a man who was being beaten and tied to a tree. He was shocked to see this, but his dad asked him to keep quiet and look the other way. This was just his first experience of visiting the village and seeing how the landlords treated their peasants.

In Kareem's own words, "My dad liked the property and asked the brokers to finalize the deal. It took several days to do it. We were housed in one of the two villas belonging to the landlords (the Quraishi brothers). Dad and some people went to see the boundaries of the property on horseback. It was a caste area."

It was almost dusk when everyone returned. There was some argument as the sellers were claiming that there was a dispute between them and Astan Quds Rezavi. The shrine of Imam Reza, the eighth Imam of Shia Muslims, has vast properties and businesses under this trust. The trust was called Astan Quds Rezavi Foundation.

The institution owned and managed vast areas, properties, and assets all around the Khorasan province. Against the advice of all present, Dad said, "Since this is a religious institute, I will forgo my rights to the section of property and issue was settled to the satisfaction of all."

The traditional relationship between the landlord and peasant farmers was like this:

The landlord would provide the land and water and advance their funds or required quantities of seeds, fertilizers, cash advances for their needs. The farmer would work the land and at the time of harvest, the landlord would be repaid for these expenses from the harvest proceeds. As far as I recall, the proceeds were to be distributed on the basis of 60% to the landlord and 40% to the farmer.

Mr. Kazem further recalls that it was a very cold winter night. "Everyone was sitting in a warm room and being served tea and snacks while the farmers were standing outside, shivering with cold. I remember that a large tree was cut that night to use as firewood for heating the room."

The accounting system appeared to be very strange. Each farmer had a stick with notches on both sides. Each notch represented an amount of money or supplies received by the farmer during the year. The figures in the landowner's books were matched with the figures in the farmers' books.

It was almost midnight when all accounts including advances to the farmers were reconciled and title deed transfer was registered. Everyone congratulated my dad as the new owner.

Dad asked, "Do I own this village now?"

"Yes, of course," they said.

Dad asked about the carpet and other things. They said, "Yes, of course. You are the owner of the entire village and everything that is here."

Gholam Hussein said, "Please ask all the farmers who are waiting outside to come inside."

There was a big murmur among those present. They said, "Now you are the owner and should not treat these farmers the way you are because you will not be able to control them."

Dad said, "I did not say a word till the transfer deed was finalized and told the farmers that henceforth, it will be partnership between me and all of you." He offered everyone tea and snacks and explained that his way of working was different, and everyone would be respected. This way, everyone would be happy and making lots of money. Dad had always preferred to work as a family and to have good cooperation with others.

The first thing that he did soon after accession was to repair the public bath house and mosque. He also opened a school. In addition to the residents of the village, people from surrounding villages also started coming to avail of the facilities that were not available in their villages. Water sources were, however, limited and the entire area could not be utilized.

Gholam Hussein spent a lot of money on the enhancement of the Qantas system to double the volume of water as irrigation was through this system. Qantas system refers to an ancient system of irrigation in Iran which allows water to be transported over long distances. It is fed through a series of wells connected by a series of underground tunnels. An expert is appointed who can detect a source of underground reservoir which could be miles away.

He also had plans to introduce handicrafts and other similar activities so that women and farmers could use unproductive winter months to learn a craft and earn extra money.

Unfortunately, the farmers and the overseer appointed by Gholam Hussein took advantage of his kindness. He and the farmers had raised sheep that was used to produce cheese, ghee, and other products. Every time the overseer came to his house, he would report that numbers of sheep belonging to the landlord were missing. Gholam Hussein was very upset because of this brazen cheating. Finally, when the harvest was ready and the overseer came to his house with accounts, the volume of harvest was far below the assessment made by the specialist earlier. Reluctantly, Gholam Hussein decided to sell the village which he had worked so hard to develop and his dreams were crushed. Instead of going for an orderly sale, he announced a fire sale and decided to return to Bombay.

The emergence of India Coffee House

Coffee in India was introduced by the British, and in order to promote it, Coffee Cess Committee (CCC) was formed by the government. This committee would assist coffee growers in selling their products.

To implement this, CCC entered into an agreement with J Walter Thompson (JWT), a world-famous advertising company, to promote their marketing. They would go around the streets with a music band with twirling girls handing out packets of coffee samples and colourful pamphlets.

Gholam Hussein had opened a restaurant on Church Gate Street, Bombay, in partnership with James, a retired army officer, under the name of Chevalier Restaurant, which was doing reasonably well. This was a typical Iranian restaurant. One of the clients, a retired army officer working for the JWT Company, had a conversation with Gholam Hussein about it when bands were passing in front of the restaurant.

Gholam Hussein said, "These people don't know how to sell coffee."

"What?" exclaimed the officer. "This is being done by a world-famous advertising company, and you say they don't know marketing.

I have been working in this company. I think if you have a better idea, you can have a meeting with company personnel." Gholam agreed to meet with an officer of JWT, Mr. Fielding.

Prior to this, coffee was considered a special drink to be served in an agreement that was signed in September 1936. The restaurant was renamed "India Coffee House." It opened at

Church Gate, Mumbai in 1936, and was operated by the Indian Coffee Board. Even though coffee had been grown by Indians since the 16th century, the idea of coffee houses as they exist today was new at the time. The 'Indianism' of this particular chain came from the fact that most coffee houses existing at the time were run by the British and discriminated against locals.

The meeting that took place between Gholam Hussein and JWT officials was very constructive and it was agreed between two parties that the name of Chevalier restaurant would be changed to "India Coffee House.". As per the terms of the agreement, JWT would pay a fee for each cup of coffee sold as well as for each pound of coffee sold. This agreement was to remain valid for one year which will be renewed by mutual agreement.

Gholam Hussein knew how to promote coffee. He placed a small coffee grinder and roaster in front of the window of the restaurant.

The scent of the coffee being roasted was like a magnet to passers-by who were invited to come in and enjoy the drink and see how it was made. Coffee was served in a beautiful jug by uniformed waiters for only 4 annas (16 annas made one rupee).

This setup proved a huge success. One of the customers who liked it much was Mr. Horniman, a leading journalist who began writing about the coffee house as a place to visit. He and his entourage of young reporters were regular visitors to the coffee house. The business was beyond their expectations.

Gholam Hussein's partner, James, did not get along well with Mr. Fielding. Mr. James did not know how to run a business, and officials of JWT were not happy with his behaviour and interference.

In a meeting that took place with JWT, they made it clear that they will renew the contract only if James is out. Gholam, however, did not want to break his partnership with James and refused to agree to their proposal so such contract was not renewed. JWT decided to open a restaurant in their banner just opposite Golem's restaurant. They rented a place and furnished it well.

But Gholam Hussein was undeterred. The restaurant was renamed Pioneer Coffee House. Customers would congratulate Gholam Hussein on his new premises, and he stood outside to explain what had happened.

JWT decided to counterattack and placed collared ads in all the newspapers with three flags – Congress, Muslim League, and British Union flags. The flags contained the slogan, "Opinions may differ, but all agree that the best place is The India Coffee House." These banners were written all over.

There was a major advertising campaign and beautifully arranged three-colour flags were displayed on the front windows of India Coffee House exactly adjacent to the door of Pioneer Coffee House. To counter this massive advertising campaign, Gholam Hussein purchased three rims of textiles – white, green and orange and had them sewn together and mounted them on a huge pole which, once raised, covered almost all the width of Church Gate. On the banner was written "United we stand, divided we fall.". Soon a large crowd gathered to see what was happening as Gholam Hussein was shouting about unity. This became big news in the town, and newspaper reporters were all rushing to Church Gate to cover, and even the radio carried the news "War of Flags."

The idea of JWT of raising three flags had completely misfired. JWT officials quickly removed the flags and decided that they had to move away from Pioneer Coffee House from Church Gate.

Pioneer Coffee House had become very famous. It was a successful operation and continued with success for a couple of years.

James, a partner in the business, continued with his usual arrogant and unprofessional approach and soon, differences between him and Gholam Hussein became glaringly obvious. At one point, it became unbearable and Gholam Hussein decided to quit. James had retired from his job with maritime and was spending most of his time in the restaurant. Gholam Hussein was trying to expand the business and stocking the supplies and equipment, but James wanted to curtail the business and insisted on procuring second-rated supplies. He also misbehaved with customers who complained to Gholam Hussein. Gholam had an argument with James, and because there was no written agreement of the partnership wherein Gholam Hussein was to be considered an equal partner, James fired Gholam Hussein, and the matter went to court.

Gholam Hussein was dejected. This was a massive setback to him, and he did not know what to do next. He had earned a good reputation and a reliable friend in his life. One day, someone knocked at his door, and there were a couple of friends at the door. Some of them were regular merchants who were regular suppliers at the Pioneer Coffee House, like the butcher, milk supplier, tea supplier, and sugar supplier.

They asked Gholam what he was doing now and what his future plans were. They insisted that he should open another restaurant.

"How can I start a new business? I have no money. All my money was in the company that has been taken away."

But his friends insisted that he must start a new business, and they offered him help in terms of cash and supplies, which could be paid back when he would be able to repay after settling down in the business.

Gholam Hussein was encouraged. He had faced this challenge many times in his life. He went out to look for a place to rent and start the business. He was able to find a place that was available and it was on Church Gate Street, incidentally, on the same building (adjacent to Pioneer Coffee House). The problem was that the landlord used the ground floor for some social services and only the third floor was available. It looked strange to have a restaurant on the third, but Gholam did not want to delay his plans, and he opened a restaurant that was name Coffee Club.

After he rented the place and purchased everything necessary to start it, he requested his friend Mr. C.K. Naidu, a famous cricketer and first Indian captain of the cricket team, to perform the opening ceremony of the restaurant. Invitations were sent to various dignitaries of Bombay, his friends, and regular customers, including Mr. B.G. Horniman (a famous British journalist).

This was a very impressive beginning of a restaurant. Slowly, business started picking up, and in a short time, it became famous. One evening, he got a phone call from the landlord.

"Are you interested in moving to the ground floor?" the landlord asked.

"Yes, of course," Gholam Hussein replied.

Gholam Hussein was very excited. The landlord offered him ground floor accommodation at the same rate. The ground floor had the same area as the third floor, and he moved everything overnight, and customers found Coffee Club on the ground floor. The business grew more and more.

This was the time of World War II, and lots of soldiers from England, Australia, New Zealand, and the United States would come to Bombay. Waiters had difficulty in understanding various dialects. Gholam Hussein came up with a novel idea. He printed special menus offering 14 different items/options at a very reasonable price. A typical menu consisted of chicken, chips, green peas, bread, butter, lemonade, tea or coffee, ice cream. The next combo would be the same in the quantity of items but without green peas, lemonade, or ice cream substituted by fish or steaks for chicken and so on.

This proved very successful, and the restaurant was always full of people, and soldiers would often wait in line. He also organized the kitchen, and the chef was assigned for different items like fish, chicken, or French fries, exclusively for each item.

The pantry would prepare bread and butter. He was able to serve large quantities of food in a short time.

While his restaurant was always full of customers, Pioneer Coffee House hardly drew any crowd. The cuisine was Indian, western, and international type. He was making a lot of money and was a prominent figure in the city.

But all this changed because of the death of his wife in Iran. He was heartbroken and decided to sell Coffee Club and moved to Iran quickly.

E MURATORE, THE ITALIAN RESTAURANT

After selling his property at the Fatehabad village in Mashad, Gholam Hussein returned to Bombay. He rented a temporary place behind Esplanade Mansion and planned to move to Poona, a nearby suburb. While at home, he started making future plans. In the meantime, he started buying and selling jewellery stones, diamond, emerald, and gold bars through a dealer named Kalidas.

He was meeting a number of businessmen and one day, he was offered a restaurant in Poona which was about 120 miles from Bombay. Poona was the summer resort for people of Bombay. During the summer, major government offices would move to Poona and special express trains like Deccan Queen operated from Bombay to Poona. A major horse race was organized resulting in large crowds coming to watch these races. Besides, Poona was also the headquarters of British Southern command. Gholam Hussein accordingly moved to Poona and rented a bungalow for himself and his three children.

Three blocks of that he was planning to buy for his restaurant needed major repair and renovations. The Bakery was known for it makes its cakes and pastries fresh daily. Their Easter Chocolate Eggs and the Mango ice cream (which was handmade) were very popular. The food was prepared by expert cooks. One of the best chefs, Ebrahim Bhai, who was brought from Bombay to supervise the large kitchen, was very talented and trustworthy. The place had Sunday afternoon dances and awards were given to the best performers. Business was going great and Gholam Hussein had a lot of friends in local politics. He got a food catering contract with the Poona Racing Society. During these times, some visiting

Arab sheiks offered to move him to Saudi Arabia. But he refused as he felt that they were not reliable people.

Because of his concept to provide good education, he enrolled his children in the best English schools. His son, Kazem Agha, along with his cousin, were getting the best education.

Agha Reza was at the restaurant to gain experience. He went to Iran to bring his new wife to Poona, and they stayed in the bungalow where his new wife enjoyed a good life. She had two children by then and soon had another baby whose name was Rezieh. Gholam Hussein also rented an apartment on Main Street for his elder sons.

This restaurant, E-Muratore, was owned by an Italian named after him. It served the best of Italian food and was famous for its exotic cuisine. The restaurant had a huge area and its own bakery and bar with a staff of over 100 waiters, with many Italian cooks and bakers. They also operated a soda fountain. There was no other restaurant in the area that could match its high standards. Gholam Hussein liked it and bought it right away after a negotiation with the owner.

Soon, after taking over the restaurant, his first initiative was to offer meals to all the staff who until now were not allowed to eat. He promised them better working conditions. The workers, however, were expecting more after getting these privileges. Gholam sensed it and being an experienced businessman, he realized that his kindness was looked upon as his weakness and workers felt that they could get more from him. They were not cooperating and slowing down the normal work.

Gholam noticed it and immediately rushed to Bombay. He contacted his old staff (waiters, cooks and other pantry hands,) about 25 persons and brought them to Poona. Mr. Kazem was co-coordinating with him and waiting for his instructions. He was told to be ready and bring over the new team to the restaurant.

This was a very subtle move and well planned to keep the business going as it had a good reputation. Any strike would have had a negative impact on business. The next morning, Gholam went to the restaurant and found that the staff was not working, and they presented him with a list of demands which included higher pay and other facilities. He had a discussion with them and asked them why they had this sudden change of attitude when he was paying them the same as before and working conditions had been rather improved by him. But workers insisted on getting higher wages.

Gholam called Kazem to bring over the team. After the failed negotiation with the workers, he declared "whoever is not interested, can leave." Some of the workers stepped aside. At that time, Kazem arrived on time and on seeing him, the workers ended the strike. The work started again uninterruptedly.

In a short span of time, E-Muratore became a huge success and business flourished to new heights. It was now an internationally acclaimed restaurant.

He also continued to buy and sell gold. He changed the pattern of this trading business. Instead of buying gold bars and keeping them secure in a bank's safe deposit box, he now would buy and sell gold through a brokerage house in Bombay.

E-Muratore was unique in its style and cuisine. It was becoming more and more popular in town. This was one of the best periods of his life. He was making lot of money. In the meantime, World War II came to an end and the British Empire was downsized. The Indian independence movement was gaining strength. Britain had suffered heavily as a consequence of the long battle in World War II and they felt that it was time for them to leave India. It had become a very difficult proposition in terms of money and administration to stay in India. They decided to quit. Jinnah, who was president of Muslim League, was able to convince Viceroy that there was a need to create a separate nation for Muslims though he was not willing for its creation. Mainly, Gandhi, Nehru, and Patel were responsible for creation of Pakistan.

Gholam Hussein with his friends at E-Muratore, Poona

Gholam Hussein with his friends enjoying at E-Muratore, Poona

Gholam Hussein with staff and workers at E-Muratore, Poona

Saif Azad, Agha Vali, Kazem Paksima and friend, at E-Muratore.

Ahmad Ghahedzade, the Manager, Gholam Hussein and Government official and some friends at E murator, Poona

Gholam Hussein at the Coffee Club in Bombay.

There were riots all over India and all of the congress leaders were detained and locked up in Poona. E-Muratore was mainly visited by British people and these developments led a sharp decline in the restaurant business.

Gholam Hussein recalled how silver prices shot up after the First World War so he invested heavily in buying silver. But during World War II, the prices of gold and silver declined sharply. Because of these developments, the restaurant had to be financed and Golem's friends urged him to sell his stock and cut his losses. He was sure that the prices of silver would go up. Kazem remembered the day when Gholam went to the restaurant's cashier to take out all the cash to be able to cover the loss.

In the next week, silver prices began to go up rapidly. In a couple of months, silver prices went up by 58%. Had he been able to hold on for a couple of weeks more, he would have profited by millions.

Gholam decided that it was time to sell the restaurant and he started looking for an alternate business. He was planning to move to Karachi.

He began negotiations in Karachi. There was a chocolate factory which was owned by the Sathe Brothers, a famous name in India. They had started another factory in Poona. At that time, there were only two chocolate factories in India. They produced chocolate from the beans. Gholam proceeded to Karachi and liked the place. He settled the terms and both agreed to swap E-Muratore with the Sind Chocolate Works. This chocolate factory is still in existence today.

Incidentally, this deal was finalized on 30th January 1948 when Mahatma Gandhi was assassinated by Nathu Ram Godse, a Hindu fanatic from Poona.

Gholam spoke to his son, Kazem, over the phone informing him that the deal had been finalized and he had taken over the chocolate factory in Karachi. Kazem was told to hand over the restaurant to Sathe's representatives. Kazem recalled that while he was in the process of handing over the restaurant to the Sathe brothers, there was news on the radio about Mahatma Gandhi having been shot dead by Nathu Ram, a Maharashtrian from Poona. Immediately, people got violent and started setting properties alight in Poona.

Mr. Sathe requested a delay in the announcement of the business deal for a few days as martial law had been imposed in Poona and there were reports of some killings of people from Maharashtra.

This was the end of his association with E-Muratore and Gholam Hussein's stay in Poona. He and his family moved to Karachi in early 1948. Gholam Hussein felt that Pakistan would be a safer place being a Muslim country. Gholam Hussein felt that moving to Karachi would be a better option.

In Karachi, he could oversee the running of a very good company named "Sindh Chocolate & Biscuit Company" which was available for exchange. The Sathe group ran this company. It was a well-known brand in those days. It had a potential scope of business as the brand was already popular in undivided India.

He made negotiations with the company and finally it was taken over by him. The company had about 100 employees. The business seemed to be going strong. He moved to Karachi with his family. This company continues to be in existence in Karachi in the name of "Sind Chocolate Works."

Soon after he took over the company, problems started cropping up. The main ingredient, choco beans, had to be imported and the government of Pakistan did not have sufficient foreign exchange to import this raw material. The company had to survive on very low production levels. The other products of the company were not much in demand. Gholam Hussein had to go to the government officials regularly to get permission to import cocoa beans but the country had its own fiscal problems and they had to bear with it.

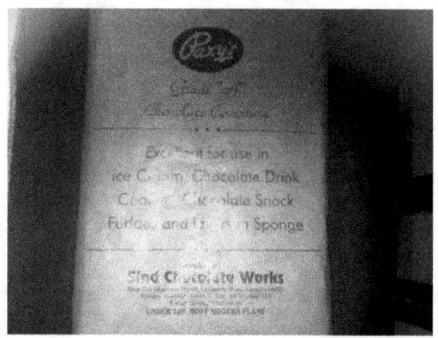

With Abid Ali, Head Chef at Sind Chocolate Works, Karachi

With Mistri Abid Ali, Plant Manager, Ebrahim Bhai, Head chef, Chowkidar Lala at Sind Chocolate Works, Karachi

Sind Chocolate Works, Karachi

*Ahmad, Manager Sind Chocolate,
Ahmad Ghahedzade and Gholam Hussein*

For seven years, starting from 1948 to 1955, the factory remained in low profile due to inadequate supply of raw material. These were hard times for Gholam Hussein and his family but he somehow managed to survive. Some of his former employees had migrated with him to Pakistan and were very loyal to him, especially Ebrahim Bhai. For many years, they worked with him with no pay. Ebrahim Bhai prepared food for the entire group. Sometimes, an old friend of Gholam Hussein, a Frenchman named Borgdome One, would come to visit him, and he enjoyed lamb chops with vegetables that Ebrahim Bhai had cooked. But now Gholam Hussein had spent all his money that he had saved. He still had his collection of books and magazines such as Geographical magazine, The Sunday Evening Post, and the Look magazine which were a saving grace. Since he was unable to pay his employees anymore, he asked them to leave but Ebrahim Bhai insisted on staying with him and so did his manager, Mr.

Ahmad Ghaedzadeh. Later, he met Ali Asghar Khan and got an invitation to join him on a visit to the city of Peshawar. He took his younger daughter, Esmat, with him. Though life was harsh, he enjoyed the rice with lamb and pink milk tea. The company Sind Chocolate Works started production again in 1955.

Meanwhile, back in Karachi, his elder siblings were in touch with Nusrat Khanum, who was settled in the oil city of Abadan and was always in touch with all others. She wanted to meet them and decided to meet them in Karachi along with Aunt Sakineh; it had been 20 years since Nusrat Khanum had last seen any of them. They arrived and persuaded Gholam Hussein that they should come to Abadan in Iran for a visit. After much persuasion, Gholam agreed. At this time, the factory once again started working normally as restrictions were lifted. The brand name "Paxy" was introduced and well accepted in the market. The products were sold to top star hotels in Karachi.

His family members had settled in Tehran and they were insisting him to join them. They finally persuaded him to shift to Iran. He sold this company in 1965 and moved to Iran.

His asked his son, Ali Agha, to come over to help him sell the place and Ali Agha arrived in Karachi soon. He sold this company in 1965 and moved to Iran.

Gholam Hussein arrived in Iran in 1965 at the age of 67. His two sons Kazem and Ali had opened the shipping company in Tehran. With the discovery of oil in Iran, the business expanded and Gholam Hussein decided to stay in Iran where he could guide his sons in business. His sons were following guidelines and business was growing.

They were staying with Nusrat Khanum. At this time, his former brother-in-law, Agha Daiee, who was on his way to visit the nearby city of Karbala, Iraq, decided to meet him in Abadan. He was sick with throat cancer. When they met, they shared old memories and Gholam Hussein promised to visit him in Mashad soon.

His elder sons had settled in Iran and his younger sons were studying in school. Ali Agha got into a partnership with a shipping company but soon opened his own shipping company. Kazem Agha who was working in Babosar also joined him.

Gholam Hussein soon bought a large piece of land. He supervised the building of a bakery and coffee shop though it was much smaller than his factory. During this time, he visited Japan in 1973 and USA in 1976. He also made two more trips in 1981 and 1984. His manager, Rustam, managed the place while he was away. Iran was going through a political unrest and in late 1978, war between Iran and Iraq prevented him from travelling further. With the exile of Mohd Reza Pahlavi, Shah of Iran and emergence of Ayatollah Khomeini in power, things dramatically changed and it had an impact in all businesses. The shipping business, which was carried on by his sons, suffered a massive blow and they had to leave Iran. They had purchased a 16000-ton ship by the name of "Peeshgaam" and launched it from Hiroshima, Japan. Their shipping company "Iran Express Lines" was going well but because of the Iran revolution, they had problems with the new government.

In 1979, Gholam Hussein visited his children in New Orleans and Houston in USA and after staying with them for one month, he returned to Iran. He also got his eye operation for cataract in 1981 in Houston, Texas and his eyesight became much better. He was able to see colours vividly.

But Gholam Hussein was always on the move and looking for new projects. In Iran, he opened up a bakery with PAXYS brand. It was a smaller unit in comparison but he was satisfied with it. He was visiting his sons regularly to different places. He continued his bakery business till the end of his life.

He always dressed immaculately and had 60 or more suits — always with a starched handkerchief. He was a person who liked to live in style.

He was rarely seen in pyjamas and would put on a freshly dry-cleaned suit every day.

He made sure that we had oatmeal (porridge) and boiled eggs for breakfast and castor oil once a month.

Association of Gholam Hussein with Key Personalities

Tay Garnett

William Taylor "Tay" Garnett (June 13, 1894 – October 3, 1977) was an American film director and writer. He used to visit Indian Coffee House and became friend with Gholam Hussein Paksima. In the process, both would discuss important social and political events.

Born in Los Angeles, California, Garnett attended the Massachusetts Institute of Technology and served as a naval aviator in World War I. He entered the film industry as a screenwriter in 1920, writing for Mack Sennett and Hal Roach, then joined Pathé and began to direct films in 1928. Among his films are *One Way Passage* (1932), *China Seas* (1935), *Eternally Yours* (1939), *Seven Sinners* (1940), *Cheers for Miss Bishop* (1941), *The Cross of Lorraine* (1943), and *Bataan* (1943). He is best known as the director of the 1946 thriller *The Postman Always Rings Twice*, starring John Garfield and Lana Turner. *A Connecticut Yankee in King Arthur's Court* (1949), starring Bing Crosby and Rhonda Fleming, was also well received. Garnett also worked in radio as a writer, director, and narrator. He created the program *Three Sheets to the Wind* (1942), which starred John Wayne as Dan O'Brien, an American private eye posing as a drunk on a luxury liner sailing from England in 1939.

Garnett directed one of Loretta Young's last theatrical films, *Cause for Alarm!*, in 1951. He travelled to the United Kingdom in the early 1950s for a few films. Upon his return to the United States, he worked mainly in television in popular series such as *The Loretta Young Show*, *Wagon Train*, *Laramie*, *The Untouchables*, *Naked City*, *Rawhide*, and *Bonanza*.

Born	William Taylor Garnett (1894-06-13)June 13, 1894 Los Angeles, USA
Died	October 3, 1977(1977-10-03) (aged 83) Sawtell, California, USA
Occupation	Film director, writer
Years active	1920–1975
Spouse(s)	Patsy Ruth Miller (m. 1929–33) Helga Moray (m. 1934–42) Mari Aldon (m. 1953)

Chiang Kai-shek- Former President of Taiwan

Chiang Kai-shek (31 October 1887 – 5 April 1975), was a Chinese Nationalist politician, revolutionary and military leader who served as the leader of the Republic of China from 1928, first in mainland China until 1949 and then in Taiwan, until his death in 1975.

During World War II, Chiang Kai-shek, as the Allies' supreme commander in China, paid an official visit to India from February 5 to 21, 1942, with the consent of the British Government. According to the available historical study, this trip of Generalissimo Chiang was very closely related to the final independence and liberty of India four years later, which had already been under almost one century of colonial rule of Great Britain. First, during his India visit, Generalissimo Chiang, being in the position of a friendly expostulator, openly appealed to the British ally to grant the Indian people their real political authority:

"Great Britain should give real political authority to the Indian people as soon as possible without waiting for a demand from the people. Of course, India's participation in this war is striving for the victory of the democratic camp against aggression, but it also is vitally related to the liberty of India herself. Objectively, I consider this to be the most enlightened policy, and it will certainly not be harmful."

It is not clear when and where my dad, Gholam Hussein, met him but in my conversations with him, he recalls having met him in Bombay at his restaurant where other prominent leaders were also present.

Mohammad Ali Jinnah

Muhammad Ali Jinnah (born December 1876 – 11 September 1948) was a barrister, politician, and the founder of Pakistan. Jinnah served as the leader of the All-India Muslim League from 1913 until the inception of Pakistan on 14 August 1947, and then as the Dominion of Pakistan's first governor-general until his death. He is revered in Pakistan as the Quaid-i-Azam ("Great Leader") and Baba-i-Qaum ("Father of the Nation"). His birthday is observed as a national holiday in Pakistan.

Gholam Hussein Paksima was having a court case in Bombay High Court with a party on business dispute and the other party preferred to have the most distinguished lawyer of India to present their case. Although the facts of the case were clearly in favour of Gholam Hussein, Jinnah twisted the facts with remarkable professionalism and won the case. Later, in a conversation with Gholam Hussein, he justified his stance that he had overturned the truth because he was paid by his opponent and it was his duty to be on their side, right or wrong.

C. K. Naydu
First Indian Tes Cricket Captain

C. K. Naidu was born on 31 October 1895 in Nagpur. He was the son of Rae Bahadur Cottari, a rich person from Machilipatnam, Andhra Pradesh, a lawyer and landlord owning several villages and sizable chunk in Nagpur. Besides being a flourishing lawyer, he was a pioneer member of the All India National Congress party.

Naydu went to England for higher studies. He had a passion for cricket and played in state level tournaments. He was a very aggressive cricketer. In order to understand his impact on Indian cricket, we have to travel back to early 1900 AD when India was ruled by the British. The British-controlled India was aggressive and iron-fisted. Any attempt to revolt was met with ruthless power and suppression. Following the massacre of Jallianwala Bagh, Amritsar in 1919, there was public resentment against British rulers. Seven years later, the England MCC team arrived in India on their maiden visit. A young man from Nagpur, C.K. Naydu, representing India, beat the MCC bowling to a pulp, hammering 11 sixers in his swashbuckling inning of 153 in 103 minutes.

The public response was euphoric. He was showered with gifts like jewels, watches, and even a motorcycle. It was at a time when the British were controlling India in a ruthless manner and show of strength in any form was not appreciated.

But Naydu had done the unthinkable by humbling the MCC attack. Again in 1933, when MCC visited India to play cricket matches, Naydu lit up the gloom by hitting furious 116 against a powerful English attack at Lahore. The English government was even more bitter and volatile. It did not like the resistance in any form, be it cricket or any other competition. But the Indian crowd was ecstatic on their hero's performance. Two young students from the crowd later wrote how his stroke play symbolised a broader political possibility. Expressing gratitude to Naydu, one wrote, "You have driven away the fear of foreigners." A second student said, "Every sixer hit by you was as good as a nail in the coffin of the British Empire. The power of your strokes was an assertion of our resolve to throw Bruisers out of India."

Naydu became a national hero. He was first captain of the Indian cricket test team and also the first Indian to feature in Wisden Cricketer of the Year in 1932.

Naydu and his cricket followers frequently visited Pioneer Coffee House in Bombay. He was a close friend of Gholam Hussein Paksima. Pioneer Coffee House also arranged coffee in the stadiums during cricket matches and private parties hosted by cricket teams. Because of his close association with C.K. Naydu, he was requested by Gholam Hussein to attend the inauguration ceremony of Coffee Club when he decided to open up his own restaurant after splitting from Pioneer Coffee House because of James' activities.

Ahmad Paksima with brother Mahmood Paksima

Naydu died in 1967 in Indore at the age of 72 but his legacy remains in the world of Indian cricket. There is a trophy in his name and a tournament was organised in India to honour this great legend. He was the first cricketer to win the Padma Bhushan award in 1955 by the government of India.

The B. K. S. Iyenger Connection

Bellur Krishnamachar Sundararaja Iyenger (14 December 1918 – 20 August 2014), better known as B.K.S. Iyenger, was the founder of the style of yoga known as "Iyenger Yoga." He was considered one of the foremost yoga teachers in the world. He was the author of many books on the practice of yoga and philosophy including *Light on Yoga*, *Light on **Pranayama**, Light on the* Yoga, Sutra of Patanjali, and *Light on Life*. Iyengar was one of the earliest students of Tirumalai Krishnamacharya, who is often referred to as "the father of modern yoga." He has been credited with popularizing yoga, first in India and then around the world. Incidentally, he was the first one to introduce yoga in USA.

The government of India awarded the Padma Shri in 1991, the Padma Bhushan in 2002 and the Padma Vibhushan in 2014. In 2004, Iyengar was named one of the 100 most influential people in the world by the *Time* magazine.

I had been able to have access to the book written by Mr. B.K.S. Iyenger, the yoga teacher, in which he has written about the advantages of following yoga. He has cited many examples and in one of his books, he has made a reference to Mr. Gholam Hussein.

He writes as under:

I was approached by the proprietor of a prestigious hotel by the name of E Muratore whose daughter Esmat was affected by polio after an injection. The proprietor Mr. Gholam Hussein Paksima asked me to take up his daughter's (Esmat) case. I agreed to try my best. She improved faster than the doctors had anticipated. Now she is a mother of three children settled in America. Her leg was affected but I made her not only walk well but ride a bicycle too..."

In the process of exploring his life events, we have gone into the details of B.G. Horniman, Editor of Bombay Chronicles and also Russy Karanjia. It was very interesting to note that three great journalists were meeting at a restaurant near Kala Ghoda, Bombay and it was there that they decided to launch a weekly newspaper named Blitz. This paper was launched in the year 1941. It was confirmed that they met at Wayside Inn restaurant where the idea of starting Blitz was formed. This restaurant was at Kala Ghoda area, close to Coffee Club Restaurant and they had been going to Coffee Club frequently.

Mr. Russy Karanjia was one of the biggest journalists in India and he had strong links with Mr. B.G. Horniman, a British reporter. Mr. B.G. Horniman, Russy Karanjia, D.F. Karaka and Dinkar Nadkarni were close friends of Gholam Hussein and they had meetings together at Coffee Club.

"Let us not divide yoga, but live in yoga to discover ourselves. Let us involve ourselves totally and wholly in the asana practice and see where our doubts take us."
Guruji BKS Iyengar

Revisiting the Roots

The village that he had left some 65 years ago was very much in his memory. The memories of his childhood friends, its streets, the scorching heat, and the house where he once lived tugged on him like a gravitational force. He finally decided to visit the village where he could once again refresh his childhood memories and meet his old friends like Pandit Suraj Mal.

It was in the year 1973 when my dad asked me to go to India with him and visit the village there. Pandit Suraj Mal was still there, running a shop with his sons and awaiting him to share their most cherished memories.

My dad, Gholam Hussein, used to tell me that "people like to look at the future and not the past." He told me about the book "Roots" written by Alex Haley, which was a bestseller in its time. He urged me to read the book and see the importance of one's past.

My dad, Gholam Hussein, had already told me, "When I found my senses in childhood, I saw my father with two cows. He and his father would put wooden rods, the yoke, to plough the fields. He described the conditions in the village and the earthquake in 1905." He talked about the caste system in India. He told me that his forefathers were from the royal family of Prithvi Raj Chauhan. Although my dad was sceptical about this, later Mr. G.S. Gill who did extensive research on the history of the Toors and other clans in India confirmed that the Toors were the descendants of the Chauhan dynasty.

Finally, my dad persuaded me to accompany him for the final visit to his ancestral village, Khosa Pando. I was excited, too, and this brought new awakening in my life to understand humanity with deeper understanding. I had an opportunity to visualise the flashbacks of my father's earliest life where all this historical and most amazing journey started and that changed our lives forever.

A Final Journey to a Native Land

My dad and I finally made a trip to India in 1973 and we reached Moga. We were treated very kindly by the villagers. Pandit Suraj Mal and his family were overjoyed and for them it was also like a dream come true. Pandit Suraj Mal was emotionally overwhelmed and hugged my dad with unimaginable passion. It was a remarkable sight to witness. Soon they started a conversation about their childhood memories.

My dad remembered his childhood days — when he used to live in the village. He enquired about the Gurudwara and the small shop near the Gurudwara that existed in the past. He ate his favourite meal – chapatti with spinach leaves curry or saag (Makki ki Roti and Sarson ka Saag). He enquired about his friend's family. He shared some pictures of his family. He told Pandit Suraj Mal that he couldn't read or write Punjabi or Hindi, but he could read and write Urdu. He described how he had to struggle in Iran, and how he established a factory manufacturing chocolate. It was difficult to get a license as the raw material had to be imported. The political situation was very adversarial and later when things changed, he managed to get a loan for 200000/- and started the factory. Again, another 300000/- was sanctioned by the government and eventually his business was established. He talked about his other friends who were in his village during childhood. He talked about Manga, Ishar Singh, Rattan Singh, Sher Singh, and Charan Singh. He had a very vivid memory of his relatives named Harnam Singh and Kala Singh. On a suggestion given by Pandit Suraj Mal, that he should come back to village and spend his retired life there, he told him that he was quite old then (around 75 years) and his children wanted him to stay with them in America. I had recorded all his conversations and I now wonder how his memory was so good. In fact, his past memories always remained in his mind all his life whether it was Iran, Karachi, or United states. It was like a gravitational pull that always reminded him of his past days.

From the conversation that my dad had with the villagers, it appeared that after leaving the village in his early years, he returned to the village somewhere in 1930 and he was there just for a couple of hours. He met one of his relatives, Kala Singh, sons of Harnam Singh. It appears that the land was in possession of Harnam Singh who was his uncle and a very honest person. Gholam Hussein's purpose to come to the village was to get the land transferred to his name but he allowed Harnam Singh to continue with his land business. The ancestral land was now transferred to his name, but Harnam Singh and his family continued to have possession of it. During his second visit to India, in 1973, he had a discussion with his friend Pandit Suraj Mal and it was apparent that he wanted to sell the land for the establishment of a school. He wanted all the children of the village to receive education in the school and he urged the parents to encourage their children to pursue education.

Gholam Hussein wanted to open a school in the village by selling 11 acres of ancestral land but he came to know that there was already a government school in the village. He was extremely happy to know this as he always felt that his village should have a school, something that he had missed in his life. He donated Rs. 5000/- to the school. Gholam Hussein told Pandit Suraj Mal that this could be his last visit to the village and it was his desire to visit his ancestral village before his death. He told Pandit Suraj Mal that he wanted his sons to visit the village as well. He said that he wanted to stay in the village for a longer time but had to return because of his family. He talked about the trees, houses, water pumps, his childhood friends and their family, school, and fields. The memories had emerged with mixed feelings and he was satisfied that he had made it before saying goodbye to the world.

Gholam Hussein enquired from Pandit about his sister who was married at Pakkhi Kalan village whose husband's name was Dhan Singh. He was curious to get more details about the family but Pandit told him that they did not have any links with the family. He further told Pandit Suraj Mal that his sons were well settled in their business and he lived his life well despite a lot of struggle in life. At the time of this visit, my dad was settled in Tehran.

The conversation of Gholam Hussein with Pandit Suraj Mal was mainly concentrated on two subjects. One was about his desire to set up a school which had already been done and the second was the publication of a book which could provide details about the history of the village. He was very delighted when he came to know that a school had already been established in the village.

As for his wish to have a book written on his village Khosa Pando, Mr. Gurcharan Gill, a scholar from Brigham Young University has written a book on the subject. The book which is in Punjabi gives a complete detail of the history of the village, its people, including those who shaped it to its present state, the warriors, and historical prominent personalities that it has produced.

Links to the Prithvi Raj Chauhan Dynasty

Incidentally, while searching for a link between the Prithavi Raj Chauhan dynasty as claimed by my grandfather who had been telling my dad that they were descendants of Prithvi Raj Chauhan, a king in 1192 AD, references to the Toor dynasty were eventually found. According to a blog on Jatt history, one researcher proved that the Toors were descendants of the Prithvi Raj Chauhan dynasty. It is stated that in the 11th Century, 1192 AD to be precise, the Prithvi Raj Chauhan family had been defeated in war by Afghan invader Mohammad Gauri and his ancestors moved to various places in Punjab and Delhi. People called them Khosas (meaning one who was lost) and the Toors and Tomers were from the Rajput clan who had converted to Sikhism in 16th Century. My dad always wanted proof from his dad about their ancestors that they were descendants of the Chauhan dynasty. He never got historical evidence, but his father was right on this issue. Going by the research on Toor caste and its associated people, it clearly supports that fact that Prithvi Raj Chauhan, the last Hindu emperor, had his descendants settled in Punjab, headed by Khosa Randhir Singh.

During the year 1979 to 1985, Gholam Hussein was mainly living in Tehran where he had set up a small bakery shop and spent his time in the shop. He frequently visited his sons in the United States and spent time with his grandchildren. His eldest son was in the shipping business and I had the privilege to get his guidance and advice while establishing the Jewish pastry brand *Chewys* in San Diego. His innovating skill and business techniques helped me substantially to make it a popular brand in the United States. His legacy stays forever.

Gholam Hussein passed away on the 19th of November 1985 in Iran. He remained a man of constant pursuits, giving inspiration to others; he was a guiding factor for his friends and siblings. He pursued his goals in life without the assistance of anyone, continued his relentless struggle, and gave his children a place in the society which would be a matter of pride for them. More than anything else, he had a human touch and great sense of friendship. He was a perfectionist to the core. His sons today have established businesses and he had always encouraged them to be more successful than he was by working hard with honesty, planning, and a clear goal.

Although, a successful entrepreneur, he continued his journey to make his children's future a secure one and was never distracted at any junction that could have prevented him from reaching the goals. He never cared for his personal comforts or stopped at any point even after achieving success.

His journey could be perfectly portrayed by Robert Frost in his poem, "Stopping by Woods on a Snowy Evening:"

> 'Woods are lovely dark and deep
> But I have promises to keep
> And miles to go before I sleep
> And miles to go before I sleep.'

Not desiring any luxuries, he was satisfied with simple living. His only fancy was to have a decent appearance, wearing nice costumes, and looking presentable at all times. But he never went after power or fame; he felt that life is best if you have peace at heart, good health, and peace in the family. The man is truly accomplished to have these blessings.

Inspired by the poem by W.H. Davis, "Truly Great," he sums up the philosophy in the words:

> *'With this small house, this garden large,*
> *This little gold, this lovely mate,*
> *With health in body, peace at heart*
> *Show me a man more great.'*

My dad would often give us quotes which were based on his personal experience and philosophy:

Try to take one step every day, if not, you may be two steps behind things:

> *A stitch in time saves nine.*
> *Never do a half job done.*

Always put things back where they belong - you will find them more easily next time:

> *Be tidy and clean -*
> *follow the straight path and be truthful.*
> *Be sincere and honest to your friends*
> *and it will make you more friends.*

A quick analysis of Gholam Husain's perceptions:

"If the path looks beautiful, find out where it leads to in its destination but if the destination is beautiful, don't worry about the path."

Gholam Hussein exactly chose to reach a promising destination which would lead to a better future life. He did not care how hard the journey was.

"Some people like daydreaming, engrossed in wishful thinking. Such people find the nights very short."

"Those who want to fulfil their dreams, they, feel days are too short."

Gholam Hussein dreamed about a better future like everyone else. But it was not just a fantasy or mere wishful thinking.

In pursuing his goals, he moved relentlessly to various places and was never distracted by temptations...

"It does not matter how slowly you go as long as you do not stop."

Gholam Hussein continued his journey and never looked back. While doing so, he had numerous obstacles and had to start again from scratch but never lost focus on his ultimate goal and he continued to move forward.

"Always do your best. What you plant now, you will harvest later."

Maybe his sons and daughters can interpret it better. His success and ultimate transformation into a well-known person is monumental history.

"You are never too old to set another goal or to dream a new dream."

There was always a quest for higher goals in life and events in the life of Gholam Hussein and it was clearly reflected in his intentions. He accepted the challenges and executed his plans with perfection despite many vicissitudes. Even during his last days, he always chose to be active in business.

"In order to succeed, we must believe that we can."

Leaving the village in recreation of a better life was not an unfounded gamble. He believed that his plans were feasible and it was this mental discernment that encouraged him to take the most significant decision.

"The starting point of all achievement is desire."

It is said that life is a crazy ride, and nothing is guaranteed. It may be true but Gholam Hussein looked at it with optimism which exceeded expectations!

E-Muratore, Poona – The Italian Restaurant

One of the most classic restaurants in India where India's elite and British officers of the highest rank felt a pride to visit. It was a symbol of luxury, exquisite cuisine, and classic grandeur.

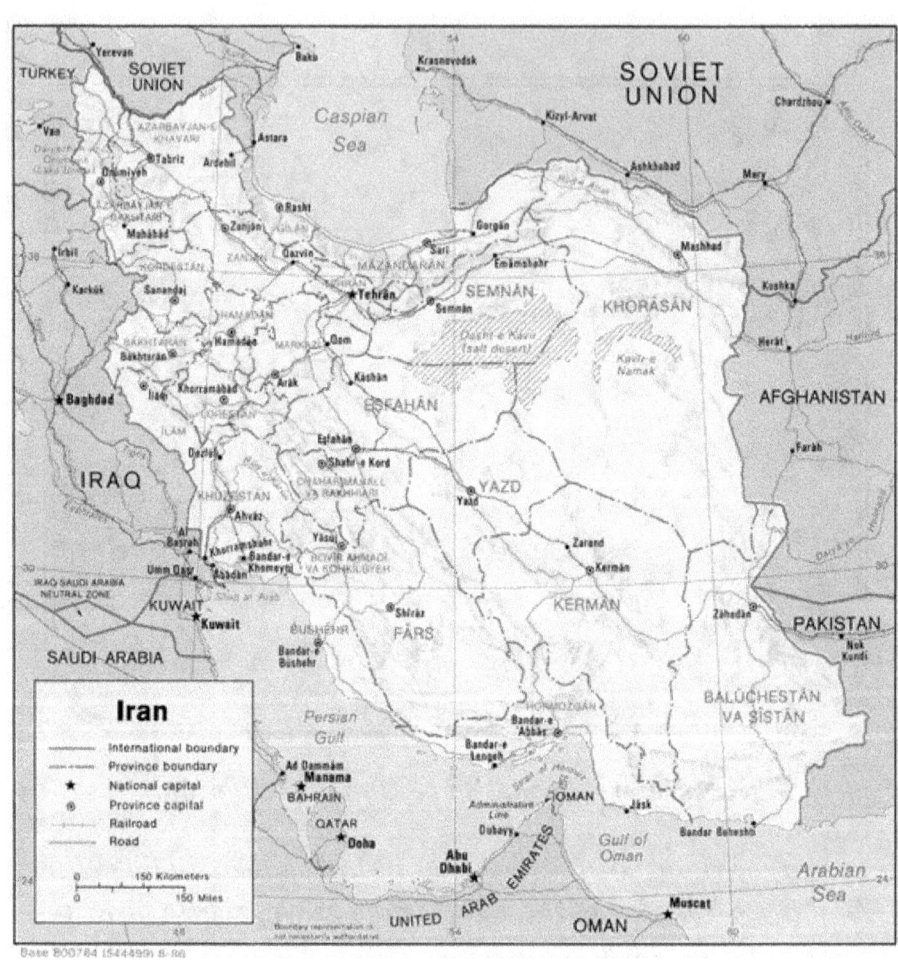

An old map of Iran

*Gholam Hussein with his wife Fatemah.
Nusrat, Kazem and children*

Nusrat, Kazem and the toddler Mahmood

Nusrat, eldest daughter in the family

Gholam Hussein and his family.

Fatemah, Gholam Hussein's first wife.

Gholam Hussein with his extended family.

Ahmad Paksima and his family

Gholam Hussein with his family

Esmat, Fatemah with Sima, Nusrat, Kazem, Gholam Hussein with Ahmad, Ali and Mahmood

Gholam Hussein in his office

Iran in 1925

Gholam Hussein with Kazem

www.ingramcontent.com/pod-product-compliance
Lightning Source LLC
LaVergne TN
LVHW011951070526
838202LV00054B/4903